Language in Society

Language in Society introduces the study of the relationship between language and society, also known as sociolinguistics, without assuming any prior knowledge of linguistics. Introducing the key concepts in an accessible way, Lee illustrates how language develops constantly as a response to society and must be understood in the context of societal norms, processes, and events. The book:

- Provides a short history of the field and explores the types of questions that can be asked in sociolinguistics as well as its methods
- Introduces essential concepts such as sociolinguistic variation, multilingualism, and contact languages
- Discusses contemporary topics including issues of language endangerment, language and justice, as well as language and computing
- Includes examples and case studies from the Asia Pacific and focuses on highlighting research from the Southern hemisphere
- Provides discussions of the future trajectory of the field and some reflection points on practical applications for each chapter

Language in Society is key reading for students studying this topic for the first time with little or no background in linguistics.

Nala H. Lee is an associate professor of linguistics at the Department of English, Linguistics and Theatre Studies at the National University of Singapore.

Routledge Guides to Linguistics
SERIES EDITOR: UMBERTO ANSALDO is Honorary Professor at The University of Hong Kong.

Routledge Guides to Linguistics are a set of concise and accessible guidebooks which provide an overview of the fundamental principles of a subject area in a jargon-free and undaunting format. Designed for students of Linguistics who are approaching a particular topic for the first time, or students who are considering studying linguistics and are eager to find out more about it, these books will both introduce the essentials of a subject and provide an ideal springboard for further study.

Titles in this series:

Language in African American Communities
Sonja Lanehart

The Study of Words
An Introduction
Lewis Gebhardt

Language, Gender, and Sexuality, Second Edition
An Introduction
Scott F. Kiesling

Sign Languages, Second Edition
Structures and Contexts
Joseph C. Hill, Diane C. Lillo-Martin and Sandra K. Wood

Language in Society
Nala H. Lee

More information about this series can be found at www.routledge.com/Routledge-Guides-to-Linguistics/book-series/RGL

Language in Society

Nala H. Lee

LONDON AND NEW YORK

First published 2025
by Routledge
4 Park Square, Milton Park, Abingdon, Oxon OX14 4RN

and by Routledge
605 Third Avenue, New York, NY 10158

Routledge is an imprint of the Taylor & Francis Group, an informa business

© 2025 Nala H. Lee

The right of Nala H. Lee to be identified as author of this work has been asserted in accordance with sections 77 and 78 of the Copyright, Designs and Patents Act 1988.

All rights reserved. No part of this book may be reprinted or reproduced or utilised in any form or by any electronic, mechanical, or other means, now known or hereafter invented, including photocopying and recording, or in any information storage or retrieval system, without permission in writing from the publishers.

Trademark notice: Product or corporate names may be trademarks or registered trademarks, and are used only for identification and explanation without intent to infringe.

British Library Cataloguing-in-Publication Data
A catalogue record for this book is available from the British Library

ISBN: 978-1-032-62149-4 (hbk)
ISBN: 978-1-032-62144-9 (pbk)
ISBN: 978-1-032-62151-7 (ebk)

DOI: 10.4324/9781032621517

Typeset in Times New Roman
by Apex CoVantage, LLC

For Robin Vellu

Contents

1	An introduction to the contents of this book	1
2	Sociolinguistic variation	22
3	Multilingualism	47
4	Contact languages	72
5	Language endangerment	97
6	Language and justice	122
7	Language and computing	148
	Short glossary of terms relating to other branches of linguistics	*172*
	Index	*174*

Chapter 1

An introduction to the contents of this book

1.1 What is sociolinguistics, and why is it important?

Have you ever noticed how you might sound different from your friends and family, even if you speak the same language that they do? Have you also wondered how you yourself may not always sound the same, depending on who you are speaking to, where you are at, or what occasion it is? I know that I sound different from my long-time friend from high school, even though we spent our childhoods in the same city and supposedly speak the same variety of Singapore English. Her voice is a higher pitch than mine is, perhaps given our physiques—I am taller than she is and plausibly have a longer vocal tract. Beyond physique, her voiceless plosives (the "p", "t", "k" sounds) in English are more aspirated (meaning that they are accompanied with a much more obvious puff of air) than mine are. My version of English is most probably influenced by the other languages that I speak, in which voiceless plosives are not really aspirated. She also uses some words differently from me. She says "pail", but I say "bucket"—a result of my having spent too many years away in the United States for graduate school. I also speak differently to her than when I speak with my community elders. I have no qualms saying "you" with her. But it is impolite in my heritage language, Baba Malay, to use *lu* 'you'. Instead, I am expected to address my community elders by their proper salutations, such as *tachi* so-and-so, *tachi* denoting 'older sister', even when I am speaking to them in English. I know I sound different yet again when I give a lecture, as compared to when I am trying to buy fruit at my local market. My voiceless plosives are much more aspirated in

DOI: 10.4324/9781032621517-1

the former context, when my speech is a lot more careful. In fact, I do all of these things in English, but some might rightfully point out that I speak Standard Singapore English when I am in lecture mode, while my business at the local markets is conducted in Colloquial Singapore English (also known in these parts as "Singlish"). Then, as a multilingual speaker curious about my own language use, I observe that I can make different language choices based on what language my interlocutor might be most comfortable with and how I want them to feel about me. I might use Mandarin with friends from China or Malay with the Malay canteen vendor at my university if I wanted them to think of me as being somehow connected to some wider social group that they are all part of. Perhaps the canteen vendor may take a liking to me for using their language, and they might give me larger food portions or an extra side! In effect, I am using language to do things. So how does it all come together? What is the role of language in society, and what is the effect of society on language? These are but some of the compelling questions that the subfield of sociolinguistics attempts to address—compelling because these questions acknowledge your role as a speaker and active participant in the wider web of things! Sociolinguistics is the study of language *in society*, essentially the title of this volume. This subfield is concerned with the dynamic interrelations between language and society. Society shapes language, and language in turn has the ability to affect what happens in society.

The study of sociolinguistics has come a long way since the 60s, during which time mainstream linguistics was dictated by the belief that you could understand a language just simply by looking at its structure. The whole idea behind generative grammar is that there is a logical set of rules that generates language output and that the human brain holds some sort of innate language faculty that does precisely this. It makes sense that the researchers who take such a stance do not think very much about the interactions between language and the environment in which it unfolds. Noam Chomsky, leading figure in generative grammar, and, these days, political commentator, is remembered for saying that sociolinguistics is not concerned about grammar. Instead, he attributed the issues underlying the types of questions that sociolinguistics was trying to address solely to the notion of power and commented that sociolinguistics could not possibly be a serious field of study. Prominent sociolinguist Suzanne Romaine recalled this in her textbook first published in the 90s, *Language in Society: An*

Introduction to Sociolinguistics (1994). Sociolinguistics has come a long way since then. In addition to the study of language in society becoming a lot more recognised and treated as a rigorous field these days, the concerns of the field itself have expanded, as have the methods that are utilised to address these evolving concerns. This is not to say that the traditional questions asked, issues raised, and methods used then were not important ones but that sociolinguistics stays very much relevant in today's society. This volume pays tribute to some of the most important ideas and the people behind them in sociolinguistics but also explores the new ground that sociolinguistics has made, for example, in the study of language endangerment (which has become a threat of exponential magnitude in today's world) and in its potential contributions to computational linguistics (which is responsible for the rise of chatbots, machine translation, speech recognition, and other tools such as these). But before understanding the role of sociolinguistics in other subfields, it would be interesting to travel back in time for a bit.

It was initially thought that Haver Currie might have been the first person to use the term "sociolinguistics" in a paper given at a conference in 1949, but the term actually appeared a decade before that in an article written by Thomas Callan Hodson in 1939. "Sociolinguistics in India", which was published in a magazine, *Man of India*, discussed language as a social means, including the importance of context in the use of language and terms of address, and highlighted tribal languages that were used in India, in addition to other topics (Hymes 1979: 141). While the Western world was not already using the term "sociolinguistics" at that time, Swiss linguist Louis Gauchat (1866–1942) made an important discovery at the turn of the 20th century. He discovered that the variation in speech found in the village he was studying (Charmey, an alpine village in Switzerland) was determined largely by social factors. His 1905 publication, *L'unité phonétique dans le patois d'une commune*, undoubtedly provided an essential basis for the development of modern-day sociolinguistics, particularly variationist sociolinguistics, which will be covered in Chapter 2.

Meanwhile, Gauchat's contemporaries were much more interested in looking at regional variation through traditional dialectology. So, what is a **dialect**? Linguists in general view dialects to be a variety of a language that is associated with a place or a region, such as the various dialects of Japan that are delineated by region, such as the Tohoku-*ben* or Kanto-*ben* (Tohoku refers to the northeast area of the main island of

Japan, Kanto refers to a region surrounding and including Tokyo, and *ben* indicates 'speech' or 'dialect'). Nowadays, the term can also be used to refer to the variety spoken by a social group, sometimes also referred to as a 'sociolect'. For instance, a well-known sociolect that originated in the 80s is Valley Girl speak, characterised in part by the high rising intonation that would accompany the end of declarative sentences and used by young, affluent women from Southern California who were largely viewed to be materialistic (if you need a reference character, the quintessential Valley Girl would be Elle Woods in the 2001 film *Legally Blonde*). Returning to the notion of a dialect, linguists in general would expect dialects to share mutual intelligibility with other dialects of the same language—meaning that a speaker of Cockney English would most probably understand a speaker of Singapore English to the extent that they would be able to communicate without impedance in the most part. Note that in the past, dialects were at one point viewed with some historicity, having been used to refer to daughter languages of a common ancestor language, but this use is no longer common. More popularly, the general public's opinion appears to be that a dialect is some non-standard, non-official, or even inferior variety of a language. For example, languages such as Hokkien, Cantonese, and Hakka are considered dialects of Chinese in China and in countries such as Singapore, even though these languages are not mutually intelligible and are actually very different from Mandarin, which forms the basis of what is referred to as 'Chinese' because of its official status in these places. These sentiments are perhaps best summed up by a renowned scholar of Yiddish, Max Weinreich (1944), who lived between 1894 and 1969. While recalling a statement made by a member of the audience at a lecture he gave, Weinreich stated, "A language is a dialect with an army and navy". Beyond dialects, yet another notion that is imprinted in public consciousness is that of accent. The term, however, is not one that linguists use very much at all. The common notion of **accent** recognises that other people speak differently than oneself and is mostly concerned with how people sound, above anything else. More often than not, the layperson might say that someone speaks with an accent if they are speaking a non-standard dialect. Notice how Standard American or British English speakers almost never get that! To the linguist, however, a dialect is much more than the way one sounds. It encompasses one's lexicon (vocabulary) and syntax (sentence structure rules), among other factors. Today, sociolinguistics encompasses a lot more than what a dialect is and what an accent is. The following sections provide a quick overview of what else you might expect in your sociolinguistics journey with this volume.

1.2 What is variation in sociolinguistics and why is it interesting?

Going beyond the dialect or the accent, Chapter 2 covers a major subtopic in sociolinguistics. 'Variationist sociolinguistics', as the name of the subfield suggests, is interested in the way language varies. It is interested in how people do not sound the same all the time and how they do not sound the same as the next person who might be speaking the same language or the same language variety. Louis Gauchat's study, introduced in the previous section, was in many ways ahead of its time. An early position in dialectology was that remote, far-flung villages like the one that Gauchat was studying would be linguistically homogenous due to lack of outside influence and that the speech of *pure* dialect speakers, usually the nonmobile, older, rural males ('NORMs' in dialectology) warranted the most attention—it was believed that their speech would be the most conservative and traditional within the region and thus the most worthy of study. It was not until the 1960s that variationist sociolinguistics really took off, attributed in large part to the work of William Labov. William Labov is a sociolinguist known for his famous New York departmental store experiment (1966), wherein he tried to analyse the speech of speakers from different social classes. He would approach random salespersons at three different departmental stores that were patronised by people of different social classes, asking them where a particular item was, prior to that having ascertained that the item he had asked for was on the fourth floor. What Labov was really hoping to look at was whether there was rhoticity in the response "fourth floor". He observed that employees at departmental stores serving customers from a higher class were more likely to pronounce /r/, while those from the other stores, particularly the store catering to the working class, were more likely to drop /r/, thereby relating rhoticity at that time to socioeconomic class in New York. In essence, variationist sociolinguistics, as Chapter 2 delves into, focuses on why and how we do not necessarily sound the same, even if we are speaking the same language or language variety, attributing most of these differences to social factors. Instead of simply looking at regional differences, one might be interested in finding out how people of different ages, genders, ethnicities, classes, and other sorts of affinities differ in their language use. Language use here refers to how one sounds, the words that one might use, and even one's sentence structures, although, just as with Labov's classic study, most variationist sociolinguists are interested in how one sounds. Of course, we are not claiming that we sound the same all the time—this depends on who we are talking to, the context and/or environment we are in, or how we are attempting to style ourselves, when these choices are available to us. Speaking of who and when, we know that speakers may have different sets of registers that they can avail of in different situations. For instance, speakers of Javanese have three broad speech levels (*ngko*, *madya*, and *krama*). *Ngoko* is non-polite, informal, and used only with inner-circle people one is very familiar with. *Madya* is a level that is halfway between polite and impolite and halfway between formal and informal, used when addressing people who are close, but not quite, "such as a neighbour who is not a close friend". *Krama* indicates the most formal, polite level of the language, which is used when addressing "someone toward whom the speaker must be distant and formal" (Poedjosoedarmo 1968: 57). While English does not share the same sort of register levels or even the same explicitness in registers, we know that the language we use for a class presentation in school is very much different from the one that we use with our friends comfortably on social media. Relatedly, extending variation to style, which you can think of as a collection of linguistic variants imbued with particular social meanings, we see that people can use languages in particular ways to respond to different aspects of a social situation (Eckert & Rickford 2001), including but not solely limited to formality and familiarity. In a much more recent study, Qing Zhang shows that rhotacisation in Beijing Mandarin is associated with a set of male urban Beijing social personae that demonstrates a cluster of *smooth* attributes related to manners and interactional styles of social transactions that conjure an image of someone who is shrewd and worldly wise. Women professionals, on the other hand, may eschew this feature, given that there is a mismatch between such a character type and that of a professional woman in international business (Zhang 2008). It becomes clear that regardless of where in the world you might be accessing this volume from, we know that the way we speak, present ourselves, and dress, or even the activities we take part in, can influence how people perceive us (more on these in Chapter 2). These are but some of the interesting issues that variationist sociolinguists explore, using mostly quantitative methods, with some qualitative investigative work.

1.3 How is 'multilingualism' perfectly normal, and how do we study it?

Chapter 3 of this book deals with an issue that is less central to variationist sociolinguistics. A lot of variationist sociolinguistic studies have in fact been focused on monolingual groups and are largely Western-centric in nature due to the languages and regions that they cover (although this volume tries to use data from a less Western-centric perspective where possible). This ignores the fact that multilingualism has been the norm in many parts of the world for a long time now. For example, the ancient Mediterranean world was known to have been multilingual since many centuries BCE (Before Common Era), and the more extensively empires (such as the Assyrians, Babylonians, Persians) developed, the more linguistically diverse these empires became (Jonker, Berlejung & Cornelius 2021). It is postulated that only much later, with the rise of nation-states, that the "one language/one culture/one nation" paradigm came to be (Pujolar 2007: 71), problematising the notion that it was rather normal for there to be more than one language in a single space at any one time. This was and is still the case, particularly in some large Western nation states. In the United States, out of 127 million people surveyed in a 2021 population census, over 75 percent reported that they speak English only (U.S. Census Bureau 2021). Such a linguistic situation firmly contrasts with that of a country such as India, which is said to encompass between 200 and 700 languages belonging to four language families, and where people are highly multilingual (Pattanayak 1990). Note that while we are using the term 'multilingualism' in the chapter's title for its broader coverage, rather than focusing solely on 'bilingualism', the issues that this chapter deals with are relevant to anyone who uses two or more languages. It is estimated that more than half the world's population is multilingual to different extents (Bialystok 2017). It is also becoming clearer than ever that there are more benefits than disadvantages to being multilingual. Experiments carried out on children show that bilingual children have better executive control cognitively (Bialystok 2011a), better multitasking abilities (Bialystok 2011b), and a Theory of Mind advantage (Schroeder 2018), which means that bilingual children can possibly better attribute mental states to others and explain the behaviours of others based on these attributed states, an advantage that has been linked to popularity in preschool and early school years (Slaughter et al. 2015). It should also become clear that there are two main perspectives from which multilingualism can be approached—societal and the individual. At both levels, the questions that can be asked are different. What sorts of language policies are in place if a country, nation, or state professes to be multilingual, and what do these policies set out to achieve? Are all recognised languages equally valued in the multilingual society? What about the languages that do exist but that do not feature in these policies? How do multiple languages come together in a functional way? The truth is, more often than not, not all languages are equally valued, and different languages are used in different contexts, known as "domains of language use" in sociolinguistics (Fishman 1965). For instance, in Malaysia, Chinese languages or 'dialects' (as in the layperson's use of the term) are used in unofficial, small businesses, and family settings among the Chinese people, while Standard Malay and English are used in high domains such as mass media, even though only Standard Malay is recognised as an official language (in Malaysia) (Coluzzi 2017). Similarly, where the individual is concerned, chances are that not all languages are spoken equally proficiently. A simple way of thinking about this might be: how much of a second or third language must you know for you to be considered a bilingual or multilingual speaker? Would you say that a person who has learnt Japanese for only a couple of semesters is multilingual? What if this person only knows the days of the week in the language? I suspect that that would simply not suffice if you were the one doing the assessing. The key point here is that proficiency in another language and thus whether one is effectively multilingual has much to do with what one is able to do in that other language/those other languages. Tangentially, on the topic of acquisition, we can also talk about how simultaneous bilingualism is different from sequential bilingualism—for the former, both languages are acquired at the same time, whereas in the latter scenario, one language is acquired later in life than the other. Other interesting questions include why and how we switch between languages within a single sentence and/or conversation (Myers-Scotton 1995). Do we do so only when we cannot find the right word in the language we are speaking, or is it because a word in that other language might be much more suitable for expressing a particular nuance? What other reasons can there be? Are we always aware of when we are codeswitching? Additionally, just as different languages may be used for different functions in society in a phenomenon we term "diglossia" (Fishman 1967), how is the entire repertoire of a multilingual speaker used across a range of different social domains? What does the term "translanguaging" (García 2009) have to do with it all? How does multilingualism shape or affect personality? Going a step further, do we have different personalities when we speak different languages? As Chapter 3 will show, the questions that someone interested in multilingualism can ask are varied, as are the approaches to answering these questions—ranging from experimental to qualitative.

1.4 On one end of the multilingual change spectrum: contact languages

With a better understanding of what multilingualism is, Chapters 4 and 5 delve into major consequences of multilingualism. In a multilingual situation, when contact is particularly intense and sustained between speakers who speak different languages, new languages can emerge. These languages are called 'contact languages'. The actual sociological circumstances and, relatedly, the amount of sustained contact leading to the language's emergence play major parts in the way these languages are labelled, these labels including 'pidgin', 'creole', and 'mixed language', among others. For instance, a pidgin is said to emerge when people of different linguistic backgrounds develop "a common means of communication" (Thomason & Kaufman 1988: 167) in "restricted contexts such as trade, forced labour, and other kinds of marginal contact" (Winford 2003: 268). Mostly extinct today, Chinese Pidgin English is an example of a pidgin that was used for communication between speakers of English and Chinese on the Southern China coast, emerging in reports around 1715 (Morse 1926) and appearing in texts by 1743 (Baker & Mühlhäusler 1991). Communication was necessary for all sorts of purposes, including trade (Bolton 2003). In fact, the word 'pidgin' itself emerged not as a label for all pidgin languages in general but as a label for this language, deriving plausibly from the way the word *business* was pronounced by the Chinese speakers, from the Cantonese phrase *bei chin* 'pay money', or from a confluence of both (Li 2011). The term 'pidgin' then went on to be used for other languages such as Tok Pisin and Pidgin in Hawai'i. Linguistically, the language that is commonly referred to as Pidgin in Hawai'i today is not technically a pidgin but a creole. The language, also referred to as Hawai'i Creole English, is a much-elaborated form of an earlier pidgin (Roberts 2000; Siegel 2000). In the late 1800s, Hawai'i saw an influx of immigrants from countries such as China, Portugal, and Japan, among other places, when the sugar cane plantations were established. The children of these labourers learnt English at school and interacted with each other in a variety of English, but this was much influenced by Pidgin English that was brought to Hawai'i as well as their own home languages, such as Cantonese and Portuguese. Over time, the language has acquired native speakers and is less variable and much more elaborated, thereby qualifying the language as a creole rather than a pidgin (although some would say that there are pidgins with native speakers, and others might prefer to not view creoles as a nativised version of a pidgin; more on these in Chapter 4). A mixed language, then, differs quite a bit from pidgins and creoles by being created in contact scenarios where at least one speaker group is highly bilingual, resulting in a mixture that is easily separable by component languages or that is far from simplified, given the highly bilingual context in which it emerged (Thomason 1997). An example of a mixed language is Gurindji Kriol, spoken in Australia. Instead of shifting completely to the dominant English-based Kriol, the Gurindji people have maintained an expression of their identity through the usage of Gurindji Kriol, which incorporates elements of Gurindji (Meakins 2008). These examples are but some instances of the contact languages that exist in the world. In addition to these types of languages, this chapter will also cover other contact languages that are less easily categorised. While you are being introduced to these languages through a sociohistorical lens, a major source of contention among those who study contact languages has to do with whether labels such as pidgins, creoles, and mixed languages correspond to particular structural types. For example, do creoles really have the "world's simplest grammars" (McWhorter 2001), and what are the implications of saying so, or otherwise? What are some of the theories behind the formation of these contact languages, particularly creoles? For instance, is creole genesis inherently part of some language bioprogramme that kicks in when children of different language backgrounds are forced to be inventive in developing a common language (Bickerton 1984)? Should the creole be viewed as a version of the lexifier (i.e. the language from which it derives the most words)? Or are the other languages in the contact scenario, known as the substrate languages, equally if not more important in determining the form of the creole? Beyond structural issues, there are other sociological issues that are also further addressed in Chapter 4. What are the functions of these contact languages today, given that the world is now very different than the one they initially emerged into? Why might some people say that contact languages are doubly threatened as compared to non-contact languages (Lee 2020)? Why might others state otherwise? As you might already be able to tell, the study of contact languages is most notable or notorious for having scholars who agree to disagree!

1.5 On the other end of that multilingual change spectrum: language endangerment

In Chapter 5, we look at the other end of the spectrum of possible changes brought about by language contact. As an extreme consequence of multilingualism, languages can become endangered and even cease to exist—this happens when a more dominant language takes over the functions and domains of a less dominant one. In that regard, we say that language shift has occurred when speakers replace the use of their original language with another language (Fishman 1964). Language shift or obsolescence is observed to have been common throughout history, especially when we consider languages such as Sumerian, Egyptian, and Etruscan (Swadesh 1948). But the rate and magnitude with which language endangerment is currently developing is rapidly accelerating. A particularly alarming estimate that was oft repeated in the 90s and the early noughties was that 50 to 90 percent of the world's languages were at risk of being lost or doomed within 100 years (Krauss 1992). More recent work on an up-to-date database shows that about every three months or so, one language loses its last speakers (Campbell et al. 2013). As early as the 1940s, Morrish Swadesh, an American linguist who specialised in historical linguistics, wrote about language obsolescence being clearly a non-linguistic issue (1948). Language endangerment and loss have nothing to do with the actual linguistic structure of the language that is lost, but rather, a language is lost due to completely sociological reasons. Yaghan, a rare language isolate (a language unrelated to any other language) that was spoken in Chile and Argentina, lost its last speaker in 2022. Once people who lived off fishing, Yaghan traditional ways were lost with the presence of settlers. The Yaghan people started to make handicrafts and do seasonal labour in the face of tourism. Alongside the loss of their traditional lifestyle and culture, the language gradually ceased to be spoken (Last Native Speaker of Chile's Indigenous Yaghan Language Dies Aged 93 2022). Broadly speaking, languages might meet their demise due to economic factors such as the lack of economic opportunity, migration, and the destruction of habitat; political, geographical, demographic, and sociocultural factors such as discrimination, repression, or even genocide; and subjective attitudes such as perceiving languages as being backwards or having low status as compared to others (Campbell 2017). Of course, since we have just talked about contact languages, we might wonder why anyone might care about the loss of languages since languages appear to be created as well. The creation of new languages and language death unfortunately do not operate within the same equation, and language loss far exceeds the number of languages that can be speciated or the discovery of any previously uncovered language (Lee 2020). Each language is also unique in its own right, and the speciation or discovery of one cannot simply replace another. The consequences of loss affect both language communities, the scientific community, and humanity as a whole (Lee, Siew & Ng 2022). Language loss is associated with the loss of cultural or ethnic identity (Tsunoda 2005). Where the speakers are concerned, language loss is known to have adverse health effects (Flood & Rohloff 2018) as well as psychological ones (Hallett, Chandler & Lalonde 2007). Language loss also results in the loss of a knowledge of prehistory when linguists are no longer able to reconstruct a culture's past based on language (Evans 2010), and linguists also lose linguistic evidence that would provide a fuller picture of what the human brain and cognition are capable of (Lee & Van Way 2016). As a direct response to the crisis, linguists are focusing their efforts on documenting and describing endangered and underdocumented languages. While documentation and description are not particularly new endeavours in linguistics, the subfield has really taken off in the last 20 years or so. It is interesting from a sociolinguistics perspective to consider what sociolinguistics brings to language documentation and description and how language documentation and description can contribute to sociolinguistics. Chapter 5 showcases how particular concepts and methods in sociolinguistics can aid in understanding the types of changes that are taking place in an endangered language or why variation might be taking place in a language being documented. Conversely, Chapter 5 also talks about how documentation and description efforts can unearth new data that offers us new perspectives in sociolinguistics. Finally, Chapter 5 deals with how linguists are getting more involved in language revitalisation projects in attempts to reverse language shift.

1.6 What is the relationship between language and justice?

Chapter 6 explores a number of ways in which language and justice are related. As underscored in the earlier chapter, not all languages enjoy equal rights. There exists the Universal Declarations of Linguistic Rights, with specific declarations on the protection of languages and their rights, focusing on upholding equality in linguistic rights and respecting such rights regardless of political differences or territorial statuses (Universal Declaration of Linguistic Rights Follow-Up Committee 1998), which is endorsed by luminaries such as Nobel Prize winners Wislawa Szymborska and Nelson Mandela. But the document has never been officially ratified. Instead, unequal rights can lead to different outcomes including the loss of languages, as we see in Chapter 5. Unequal language rights also means that the opportunities accorded to speakers of different languages are not always the same. For example, the ability to speak a major language provides that speaker with economic opportunities that a speaker of a less major language may not have. In a vicious cycle, the less-dominant language becomes less spoken, causing it to be further minoritised, leading to further problems that language endangerment can bring (see Chapter 5). What, then, could the role of the sociolinguist possibly be in these circumstances? On a separate and yet related note, when does language become a matter of dispute? On one hand, there are cases wherein language crimes can be committed, such as with solicitation, conspiracy, bribery, threatening, and perjury, among others (Tiersma & Solan 2012). On the other hand, people can be treated unjustly on the basis of language. A famous case from the 1980s comes to mind. As a linguistics professor in Hawai'i, Charlene Sato testified at a trial in which James Kahakua and George Kitazaki accused the National Weather Service of discrimination, because it had refused to hire the two men on the basis of their accents. Sato established that the two men spoke Standard Hawai'i English, which was a variety of Standard English spoken by most educated professionals native to Hawai'i, but ultimately the trial judge ruled against them, because he did not believe that Standard Hawai'i English was a legitimate variety of English (Yokota 2008). A much more recent case shows how the knowledge of linguistics can be used to further understand certain biases in legal proceedings. Trayvon Martin was a 17-year-old African American who was fatally shot by George Zimmerman, a member of a community watch who prior to shooting him had reported him to the police as being "suspicious". A key witness in the crime was Rachel Jeantel, an African-American whose testimony was unfortunately dismissed on the account of her speech being incomprehensible, and as a result, she was deemed not credible. In actual fact, sociolinguists John R. Rickford and Sharese King demonstrated that Rachel Jeantel spoke in a systematic African American Vernacular English, with plausible Caribbean influence (Rickford & King 2016). She was far from the unreliable witness that the courts made her out to be. In other cases, sociolinguistics may plausibly be used to serve justice. An established subfield of interest here is forensic linguistics, in which the forensic linguist uses their knowledge of linguistics to aid the settlement of disputes, legal cases or proceedings that hinge upon issues of language (Olsson 2008). In a case from the United Kingdom, a man allegedly received two SMS messages from his wife who was missing. A business tycoon with whom she was having an affair was interviewed, during which he claimed that he had not seen her and that she had sent him an SMS. John Olsson, a forensic linguist, observed that the businessman had used a period instead of a comma where commas usually appear in a letter that he had written and that the missing woman's SMS to him contained the same punctuation quirk. He also discovered that the businessman used similar sorts of phrases in his police interview as in the SMS messages that the woman had supposedly sent to her husband and that these phrases were extremely rarely used by others in general. The businessman was confronted with the evidence and finally convicted of her murder. As these examples show, the ways in which language and justice are intertwined are plenty, and the topics involved can be a fruitful area of discovery for those interested in sociolinguistics.

1.7 And finally, what is the relationship between language and computing?

Yet another highly relevant area in recent years is the study of language and computing. In 2023, the public version of World Wide Web as we know it turned 30 (Ring 2023), a relatively young age in the overall scheme of things. The world has become increasingly connected through computer-mediated communication, instant messaging, and the rise of social media over various platforms such as Facebook, Instagram, and TikTok, also indicating new ways and venues in and over which language can be used. How does sociolinguistics feature in online communication across the digital sphere? The written text format and digital methods have provided researchers corpora that can easily go upward of 1 million words to hundreds of millions of words in size. In the Asia Pacific, an interesting 6.9 million-word monitor corpus that collects online texts messages is the Corpus of Singapore English Messages (CoSEM) (Gonzales et al. 2023). Using such a corpus, sociolinguists can identify patterns in the way sociolinguistic variants are used, with an extensive amount of data. Additionally, it is clear that social media provides a venue for new linguistic forms and meanings. A study on the impact of social media on the linguistic and communicative practices in post-socialist countries, including Bosnia and Herzegovina, Serbia, and Mongolia, shows that linguistic innovations are used by social media users to uphold their own values and sociolinguistic practices (Tankosić & Dovchin 2023). Beyond the sociolinguistics of online communication, computational tools themselves have been used to aid tasks that sociolinguists have to carry out. For instance, sociolinguists who study speech production may face the daunting task of transcribing hundreds of hours of spoken data or more, aligning the transcripts to the audio recordings, and segmenting the audio stream so that they are able to find particular instances of a speech sound, word, phrase, or sentence in a large set of data more easily. Forced alignment is a process in which transcriptions are aligned to audio stream automatically by using algorithms that are trained on a sizeable amount of data and often a pronunciation dictionary. Relatedly, how does the knowledge of sociolinguistics feature in computing itself, particularly with the rise of automation in computing? Computational tools such as machine translation, speech recognition, sentiment analysis, and chatbots, among others, all face issues to do with variation. These are all tasks that involve natural language processing

(NLP) or natural language understanding (NLU). Language is inadvertently variable, as these chapters, particularly Chapter 2 on variationist sociolinguistics, will show. Oftentimes, the success of these tools depends on the data that they have been trained on. For some tools, recognising variation may be more crucial than others. How well would a speech recognition tool work if the only English it ever heard was standard American English, bearing in mind that there are not only very different dialects and varieties of English but also different registers involved even for American English and so many different ways of expressing oneself that go beyond dialects and registers? Your guess is as good as mine. Beyond what sociolinguistics can possibly do for advancing computational tools, yet another fruitful area of research is looking at human–computer interaction, particularly with the rise of chatbots. Research shows that human beings do interact with computer systems as though they are real social agents. Humans are shown to apply similar sorts of social rules and expectations to computers, even to the extent of applying gender stereotypes to computers and ethnically identifying with computers (Nass & Moon 2000). Humans do all of these things, even though they recognise that computers are not human (Nass, Steuer & Tauber 1994). With the prevalence of computers, as well as huge advancements in artificial intelligence (AI) and the development of powerful tools such as chatbots (especially with the rise of ChatGPT), it becomes relevant to ask if computers are indeed social actors (Lang et al. 2013). This chapter addresses some of the more pertinent sociolinguistic issues of modern tech.

From Javanese registers to a pidgin spoken off the coast of Southern China, and from using SMS messages to help solve crime to understanding language use through the analysis of online text messages, the topics that sociolinguists cover are broad and varied. And as the chapters will go on to show, the methods with which these topics are explored are similarly broad and varied, using both quantitative and qualitative means. With this quick whirlwind tour of the main topics that this volume will explore, I hope I have piqued your interest enough in the subfield of sociolinguistics, in which we are all essentially important actors.

References

Baker, Philip & Peter Mühlhäusler. 1991. From business to Pidgin. *Journal of Asian Pacific Communication* 1. 87–115.

Bialystok, Ellen. 2011a. Reshaping the mind: The benefits of bilingualism. *Canadian Journal of Experimental Psychology/Revue canadienne de psychologie expérimentale. US: Educational Publishing Foundation* 65(4). 229–235. https://doi.org/10.1037/a0025406.

Bialystok, Ellen. 2011b. Coordination of executive functions in monolingual and bilingual children. *Journal of Experimental Child Psychology* 110(3). 461–468. https://doi.org/10.1016/j.jecp.2011.05.005.

Bialystok, Ellen. 2017. The bilingual adaptation: How minds accommodate experience. *Psychological Bulletin* 143(3). 233–262. https://doi.org/10.1037/bul0000099.

Bickerton, Derek. 1984. The language bioprogram hypothesis. *Behavioural and Brain Sciences* 7(2). 173–221.

Bolton, Kingsley. 2003. *Chinese Englishes: A Sociolinguistic History*. Cambridge: Cambridge University Press.

Campbell, Lyle. 2017. On how and why languages become endangered: Reply to Mufwene. *Language* 93(4). e224–e233. https://doi.org/10.1353/lan.2017.0066.

Campbell, Lyle, Nala Huiying Lee, Eve Okura, Sean Simpson & Kaori Ueki. 2013. New knowledge: Findings from the catalogue of endangered languages. *Talk presented at the 3rd International Conference on Language Documentation and Conservation*, University of Hawai'i at Mānoa. http://scholarspace.manoa.hawaii.edu/handle/10125/26145. (25 December, 2021).

Coluzzi, Paolo. 2017. The vitality of minority languages in Malaysia. *Oceanic Linguistics*. University of Hawai'i Press 56(1). 210–225.

Eckert, Penelope & John R. Rickford (eds.). 2001. *Style and Sociolinguistic Variation*. Cambridge: Cambridge University Press.

Evans, Nicholas. 2010. *Dying Words: Endangered Languages and What They Have to Tell Us*. Malden, MA: Wiley-Blackwell.

Fishman, Joshua A. 1964. Language maintenance and language shift as a field of inquiry: A definition of the field and suggestions for its further development. *Linguistics*. De Gruyter Mouton 2(9). 32–70. https://doi.org/10.1515/ling.1964.2.9.32.

Fishman, Joshua A. 1965. Who speaks what language to whom and when? *La Linguistique* 1(2). 67–88.

Fishman, Joshua A. 1967. Bilingualism with and without diglossia; diglossia with and without bilingualism. *Journal of Social Issues* 23(2). 29–38. https://doi.org/10.1111/j.1540-4560.1967.tb00573.x.

Flood, David & Peter Rohloff. 2018. Indigenous languages and global health. *The Lancet Global Health*. Elsevier 6(2). e134–e135. https://doi.org/10.1016/S2214-109X(17)30493-X.

García, Ofelia. 2009. Education, multilingualism and translanguaging in the 21st century. In Tove Skutnabb-Kangas, Robert Phillipson, Ajit K. Mohanty & Minati Panda (eds.), *Social Justice through*

Multilingual Education, 140–158. Multilingual Matters. https://doi.org/10.21832/9781847691910-011.

Gauchat, Louis. 1905. *L'unité phonétique dans le patois d'une commune*. M. Niemeyer.

Gonzales, Wilkinson Daniel Wong, Mie Hiramoto, Jakob R. E. Leimgruber & Jun Jie Lim. 2023. The Corpus of Singapore English Messages (CoSEM). *World Englishes* 42(2). 371–388. https://doi.org/10.1111/weng.12534.

Hallett, Darcy, Michael J. Chandler & Christopher E. Lalonde. 2007. Aboriginal language knowledge and youth suicide. *Cognitive Development* 22(3). 392–399. https://doi.org/10.1016/j.cogdev.2007.02.001.

Hymes, Dell. 1979. The origin of "sociolinguistics". *Language in Society*. Cambridge University Press 8(1). 141.

Jonker, Louis C., Angelika Berlejung & Izak Cornelius (eds.). 2021. *Multilingualism in Ancient Contexts: Perspectives from Ancient Near Eastern and Early Christian Contexts*. 1st edition. Stellenbosch: African Sun Media. www.jstor.org/stable/j.ctv1nzfzj0. (27 June, 2023).

Krauss, Michael. 1992. The world's languages in crisis. *Language* 68(1). 4–10.

Labov, William. 1966. *The Social Stratification of English in New York City*. Washington, DC: Center for Applied Linguistics.

Lang, Helmut, Melina Klepsch, Florian Nothdurft, Tina Seufert & Wolfgang Minker. 2013. Are computers still social actors? In *Human Factors in Computing Systems*, 859–864. https://doi.org/10.1145/2468356.2468510.

Last Native Speaker of Chile's Indigenous Yaghan Language Dies Aged 93. 2022. Last native speaker of Chile's indigenous Yaghan language dies aged 93. *Buenos Aires Times*. Buenos Aires. www.batimes.com.ar/news/latin-america/last-native-speaker-of-chiles-indigenous-yaghan-language-dies-aged-93.phtml. (18 July, 2023).

Lee, Nala H. 2020. The status of endangered contact languages of the world. *Annual Review of Linguistics* 6(1). 301–318. https://doi.org/10.1146/annurev-linguistics-011619-030427.

Lee, Nala H., Cynthia S. Q. Siew & Nadine H. N. Ng. 2022. The network nature of language endangerment hotspots. *Scientific Reports*. Nature Publishing Group 12(1). 10803. https://doi.org/10.1038/s41598-022-14479-1.

Lee, Nala Huiying & John Van Way. 2016. Authors' response. *Language in Society* 45(2). 301–303. https://doi.org/10.1017/S0047404515000986.

Li, Michelle. 2011. *Chinese Pidgin English and the Origins of Pidgin Grammar*. Hong Kong: The University of Hong Kong PhD dissertation.
McWhorter, John H. 2001. The world's simplest grammars are creole grammars. *Linguistic Typology* 5. 125–126.
Meakins, Felicity. 2008. Land, language and identity: The sociopolitical origins of Gurindji Kriol. In Miriam Meyerhoff & Naomi Nagy (eds.), *Social Lives in Languages—Sociolinguistics and Multilingual Speech Communities: Celebrating the Work of Gillian Sankoff*, 69–94. Amsterdam: John Benjamins. https://espace.library.uq.edu.au/view/UQ:219382. (18 January, 2019).
Morse, Hosea Ballou. 1926. *The Chronicles of the East India Company, Trading to China 1635–1834*. Harvard University Press.
Myers-Scotton, Carol. 1995. *Social Motivations for Codeswitching: Evidence from Africa* (Oxford Studies in Language Contact). Oxford/New York: Oxford University Press.
Nass, Clifford & Youngme Moon. 2000. Machines and mindlessness: Social responses to computers. *Journal of Social Issues* 56(1). 81–103. https://doi.org/10.1111/0022-4537.00153.
Nass, Clifford, Jonathan Steuer & Ellen R. Tauber. 1994. Computers are social actors. *Human Factors in Computing Systems*, 72–78. https://doi.org/10.1145/191666.191703.
Olsson, John. 2008. *Forensic Linguistics: An Introduction to Language, Crime and the Law*. London/New York: Continuum Press.
Pattanayak, Debi Prasanna. 1990. *Multilingualism in India*. Clevedon/Philadelphia: Multilingual Matters.
Poedjosoedarmo, Soepomo. 1968. Javanese speech levels. *Indonesia* 6. 54–81.
Pujolar, Joan. 2007. Bilingualism and the nation-state in the postnational era. In Monica Heller (ed.), *Bilingualism: A Social Approach* (Palgrave Advances in Linguistics), 71–95. London, UK: Palgrave Macmillan. https://doi.org/10.1057/9780230596047_4.
Rickford, John R. & Sharese King. 2016. Language and linguistics on trial: Hearing Rachel Jeantel (and other vernacular speakers) in the courtroom and beyond. *Language* 92(4). 948–988. https://doi.org/10.1353/lan.2016.0078.
Ring, Julian. 2023. 30 years ago, one decision altered the course of our connected world. *NPR*, sec. Technology. www.npr.org/2023/04/30/1172276538/world-wide-web-internet-anniversary. (2 August, 2023).
Roberts, Sarah J. 2000. Nativization and the genesis of Hawaiian Creole. In John H. McWhorter (ed.), *Language Change and Language Contact in Pidgins and Creoles* (Creole Language Library),

257. John Benjamins Publishing Company. https://doi.org/10.1075/cll.21.10rob.

Romaine, Suzanne. 1994. *Language in Society: An Introduction to Sociolinguistics*. 1st edition. Oxford/New York: Oxford University Press.

Schroeder, Scott R. 2018. Do bilinguals have an advantage in theory of mind? A meta-analysis. *Frontiers in Communication* 3. www.frontiersin.org/articles/10.3389/fcomm.2018.00036. (27 June, 2023).

Siegel, Jeff. 2000. Substrate influence in Hawai'i Creole English. *Language in Society* 29(2). 197–236.

Slaughter, Virginia, Kana Imuta, Candida C. Peterson & Julie D. Henry. 2015. Meta-analysis of theory of mind and peer popularity in the preschool and early school years. *Child Development* 86(4). 1159–1174. https://doi.org/10.1111/cdev.12372.

Swadesh, Morris. 1948. Sociological notes on obsolescent languages. *International Journal of American Linguistics* 14. 226–235. https://doi.org/10.1086/464009.

Tankosić, Ana & Sender Dovchin. 2023. The impact of social media in the sociolinguistic practices of the peripheral post-socialist contexts. *International Journal of Multilingualism*. Routledge 20(3). 869–890. https://doi.org/10.1080/14790718.2021.1917582.

Thomason, Sarah G. 1997. A typology of contact languages. In Arthur K. Spears & Donald Winford (eds.), *The Structure and Status of Pidgins and Creoles*, vol. 19, 71–90. Amsterdam/Philadelphia: John Benjamins Publishing Company.

Thomason, Sarah G. & Terrence Kaufman. 1988. *Language Contact, Creolization, and Genetic Linguistics*. Berkeley/Los Angeles: University of California Press.

Tiersma, Peter M. & Lawrence M. Solan. 2012. The language of crime. In Lawrence M. Solan & Peter M. Tiersma (eds.), *The Oxford Handbook of Language and Law*, 340–353. Oxford University Press. https://doi.org/10.1093/oxfordhb/9780199572120.013.0025.

Tsunoda, Tasaku. 2005. *Language Endangerment and Language Revitalization: An Introduction*. Berlin: Mouton de Gruyter.

Universal Declaration of Linguistic Rights Follow-Up Committee. 1998. *Universal Declarations of Linguistic Rights*. Barcelona: Institut d'Edicions de la Diputació de Barcelona. https://culturalrights.net/descargas/drets_culturals389.pdf. (29 June, 2023).

U.S. Census Bureau. 2021. *American Community Survey Supplemental Estimates: Households*. https://data.census.gov/table?q=language. (23 June, 2023).

Weinreich, Max. 1944. YIVO Bleter (Vol. 23, nr. 3) (In Yiddish).

Winford, Donald. 2003. *An Introduction to Contact Linguistics*. Oxford: Blackwell Publishing.

Yokota, Thomas. 2008. The "Pidgin problem": Attitudes about Hawai'i Creole. *Educational Perspectives* 31(1–2). 22–29.

Zhang, Qing. 2008. Rhotacization and the 'Beijing smooth operator': The social meaning of a linguistic variable. *Journal of Sociolinguistics* 12(2). 201–222. https://doi.org/10.1111/j.1467-9841.2008.00362.x.

Chapter 2

Sociolinguistic variation

2.1 What is the study of speech variation?

Before William Labov's famous New York department store experiment (see Chapter 1), he had previously carried out work on Martha's Vineyard (Labov 1963), an island off the southeastern coast of Massachusetts, USA. Traditionally fishermen, the islanders began seeing an influx of tourists from the 1960s. During that time, Labov observed that two sets of diphthongs (sequences of two vowel sounds in the same syllable) were undergoing an interesting change. In the past, the islanders had been moving towards standard American English norms in their pronunciation of the diphthongs in words such as "right" and "house" with their realisation of /ai/ and /au/ (think AY and OW), but he realised that there was a group that were pronouncing these as [əi] and [əu], the [ə] in these instances being centralised vowels that sound like UH. What happened here was that there really were two groups of people: those who identified themselves as native "Vineyarders", who rejected the values and hence representative speech style of the mainland, versus those who did not mind the tourists. The fishermen themselves, who represented the island's traditional way of life, were the ones who subconsciously rejected the mainland speech norms the most in their centralisation of these diphthongs. Young men, particularly between the ages of 31 and 45, also tended to centralise their diphthongs, as did those who lived in more rural parts of the island. What this study established clearly was that **phonological variants** (or variants attributed to the sound system of the language) could be used in ways to construct and express social meaning, which is separate from denotational meaning (another way of saying the literal meaning

DOI: 10.4324/9781032621517-2

that you would usually find in a dictionary). What this study also established was that various types of social categories and affiliations could influence one's speech production in determining which variant was produced.

Observer's paradox and the sociolinguistic interview

The **observer's paradox** is a situation in which speakers behave differently when they become aware that someone else (such as the researcher) is observing them (Labov 1972a). This means that the observations that are made in such a situation are inherently inauthentic and thus problematic. Of course, there are also huge ethical issues involved by not saying anything at all and stalking people to observe them!

The sociolinguistic interview is devised as a way of getting around the observer's paradox. The method that Labov utilised in studies such as Martha's Vineyard was a relatively open-ended sort of interview that encourages participants to include words that contained the vowels which were of interest to his study. He did not want a stilted formal reading list that would be unnatural and that might have influenced the participants to prefer one variant over another. He also did not want participants to figure out what it was he was studying, so that, again, the data would not be unnecessarily compromised.

Modern sociolinguistic interviews, following Labov (1984), focus on eliciting natural-sounding conversational speech between an hour and two hours in length, in addition to using various word lists and reading passages and eliciting information regarding one's demographic background, including items such as age, gender, ethnicity, and family background, among others. The main conversation would usually precede any of the other components so that its naturalness would again not be affected by the later components. The sociolinguistic interview can take place over two or even three sessions, just because of how in depth it is!

> Some interesting examples of questions that have been used by Labov include:
>
> Have you ever been in a situation where you were in serious danger of getting killed?
> Going back to the time when you were a kid, 10–12 years old, what were some of the games you used to play after school on the street (or in a lot)?
>
> Note that many of these questions were designed to be open ended, to elicit conversation—but of course, personal, prying questions or questions that pose a value judgement on a particular topic are a no-no (Tagliamonte 2006). If you had to design your own questions for use in a sociolinguistic interview, what would they be? Let's think a bit more critically. If you had to design an interview for people your age, what sorts of questions would you ask them to get them talking at length? Remember, you want your respondents to do most of the talking, not yourself.
>
> There are now many ways through which a sociolinguist may gather data to make meaningful deductions and inferences about how language works, but the sociolinguistics interview remains an important method.

2.2 The linguistic variable and variation

The **linguistic variable** can be thought of as one of the many ways in which a word sound, a word, or even a sentence can be said, keeping denotational or literal meaning constant. Linguistic variables vary for different reasons, plausibly indicating social class, gender, ethnicity, age, geographical region, affiliation, and more. A variable is understood to be a form that is commonly used and quantifiable (Labov 1966). In general, these would be forms that are found distributed with another form or forms (Sankoff & Thibault 1981). Debates exist surrounding the structural level at which the variable exists. One of the earliest definitions of a variable was that it was "two or more ways of saying the same thing" (Labov 1972b). In that regard, a strict view of what it meant to say the same thing would only permit phonology-type variants. For example, there would be no two ways about understanding that [kæt] or [kætʰ] refers to the furry feline animal with whiskers, even though the latter way of saying the word involves a clearly aspirated [t] (meaning that the sound is accompanied by an obvious puff of air). The same cannot be easily said of larger structural units. In Singapore English, one can say "It is like that, is it?" One can also say in a more standard way: "It is like that, isn't it?" The crucial question, then, is whether these two sentences are inherently the same in their literal meanings. A wider definition of the variable that would permit the consideration of larger sorts of structures is provided by Sankoff and Thibault's (1981: 208) approach, which requires that the variants have "generally, similar discourse functions" rather than completely identical semantic functions. Following this logic, variables can be found at different levels of a language structure, even though the ones that most sociolinguistic studies have been concerned with are phonological variables. Whether true variants outside the realm of phonology exist remains debatable, but what is clear is that language can be used to construct social meaning at all levels.

2.2.1 Examples of phonological variation

Phonology deals with the system of speech sounds in a language. An example of a phonological variant is the tapped and trilled prevocalic /r/ in Singapore Tamil speakers of English. Due to transfer from Tamil, tapped and trilled prevocalic /r/ has been a way of indexing Indian identity among Tamil Singaporeans when they speak English and is still used for these speakers to perform the Indian ethnic identity but is generally eschewed in favour of the approximant /r/ among younger speakers, the approximant /r/ being more associated with mainstream Singapore English (Starr & Balasubramaniam 2019). On a separate but related note, postvocalic rhotic /r/ appears to be indicative of higher education levels and socioeconomic status in Singapore English (Tan 2012), whereas no corresponding trend is found in Malaysian English (Pillai 2015).

A note on the many different /r/s

'Prevocalic' simply means before the vowel (e.g. 'crash'), and 'postvocalic' (e.g. 'sharp') means after the vowel. A rhotic /r/ is an /r/ that is performed quite explicitly, or pronounced, if you will, whereas a non-rhotic /r/ is one that appears to have been dropped. Standard British English is non-rhotic post-vocalically, whereas General American English is generally rhotic (think caH versus caR for the automobile). A tapped /r/ is one of the many ways in which /r/ can be pronounced; it is produced by literally tapping the tip of the tongue very quickly on the alveolar ridge, the bony ridge just behind your upper teeth. A trilled /r/ is produced with several quick contacts, as though the tongue is vibrating in some sense. The many realisations of /r/ make it a fertile resource for sociolinguistic variation.

2.2.2 An example of morphological variation

Beyond phonology, variation can be found at the level of morphology as well—**morphology** being the study of how minimal units of meanings are combined to make up words. An example of a variationist study with a morphological dimension is that of Gonzales (2023). He studies a contact phenomenon called Lánnang-uè (also sometimes referred to as Philippine Hybrid Hokkien), which is used by a minority ethnic group of mixed southern Chinese and Filipino cultural heritage. Lánnang-uè has a unique nominal derivational affixation system, in which simple Tagalog prefixes can be attached to a lexical base derived from Hokkien, Tagalog, or English. For example, the pag^{22}ka^{22} "manner prefix, derived from Tagalog" and ts^{h}am^{33} "mix, derived from Hokkien" indicates 'manner of mixing'. Using an acceptability judgement task (where speakers judge whether or not what they hear and read is well formed in their language), Gonzales (2023) shows that even though the system is widespread and highly stable, there was some sociolinguistic variation—young female speakers appeared to conform to this pattern of affixation more than older male speakers, who appeared to be suppressing their knowledge of this pattern to preserve the "purity" of their Hokkien. In the same vein, those with positive attitudes towards mixing were also more likely to conform to these patterns of affixation that involved high levels of mixing.

The acceptability judgement task

The **acceptability judgement task**, also known as the grammaticality judgement task, is not unique to sociolinguistics. It is also used in other key areas of linguistics, such as phonology, morphology, syntax (the study of sentence structure), and even semantics (the study of meaning) to figure out if a language structure is acceptable to the speaker of that language. The acceptability judgement task is also used in fields of language acquisition and even attrition, among others—popularly used because it is relatively easy to implement, and empirical data can be collected quickly. In it, a stimulus (such as in the form of sentences) is presented to participants, and participants are asked to rate the acceptability of these stimulus. Participants may be asked to choose between a simple "yes" and "no" (and sometimes "can't decide") or rate the acceptability on a Likert scale of 1 to 5 or 1 to 7 (with the higher numbers usually corresponding to top boundaries of acceptability and vice versa). One of the largest drawbacks regarding the acceptability judgement task is simply that self-assessments or reporting can be problematic. Humans may think they act different from how they behave in real life. One way in which this potential problem is mitigated is to provide enough filler questions, questions that test something else than what the actual research question is concerned with, in hopes that the participant is distracted and will thus not be overtly aware of what is actually being tested.

2.2.3 An example of syntactic variation

An interesting study is that of Cheshire (2005) who looked at syntactic variation along the dimensions of gender and social class using a corpus of speech collected from 96 adolescent speakers in the English towns of Hull, Milton Keynes, and Reading. While there was no sociolinguistic variation in her findings regarding the use of discourse strategies that were used to mark information that was new to the discourse, she did find that gender and class differences played roles in the usage of noun phrases that were not marked. In fact, working-class female adolescents tended to not mark their noun phrases in any special way when introducing these noun phrases as new information in their discourse, while the male adolescents, particularly the middle-class male speakers, tended to mark out information that was new in their discourse in more specific ways. An example that Cheshire (2005) uses is how a male adolescent with an academic parent went from saying his father had "everyone up [there]" to more specifically saying "he's got lots of uh friends at work" within the same turn. By changing the course of his sentence midway and providing details that "everyone" is actually "lots of uh friends", the speaker is marking out this information for his interlocutors to focus on. Cheshire alludes back to a previous study that suggested that girls paid more attention to constructing an interpersonal relationship with their interlocutor, whereas boys were generally aiming to be cooperative interviewees who would ask for and give specific sorts of information (Cheshire & Williams 2002). She also highlights that the working-class approach to talk construction is more collaborative, as speakers permit their interlocutors to make their own conclusions and interpretations. Taken together, the linguistic patterns involved in marking new information then appear to contrast strongly between female working-class adolescents and male middle-class adolescents.

The linguistic corpus

A **corpus** is an extensive collection of texts that have been put together in a principled way and computerised so that they are easily searchable and hence usable. By "principled", we mean that they may have been collected around a central theme or collected from a certain group of people or in a particular genre, and so on and so forth. For example, the Corpus of Contemporary American English (COCA) aims to be representative of American English and collects text from genres including spoken, fiction, popular magazines, newspapers, academic texts,

TV and movie subtitles, blogs, and other webpages. The Corpus of Singapore English Messages (CoSEM) is yet another example of a corpus, one that collects online text messages produced by speakers of Singapore English. A corpus can also comprise more data from more than one language, such as the Tokyo University of Foreign Studies Asian Language Parallel Corpus (TALPCo), which collects Japanese sentences and their translations into Burmese, Malay, Indonesian, and English. They can range in sizes. For example, COCA has 1.1 billion words, while CoSEM has 6.9 million words. Corpuses or corpora exist because they provide ways of doing many things, including providing empirical data for variationist type studies, accountability for the sorts of things we say in linguistics, justification for the types of definitions that we see in concordance-based dictionaries, such as the Collins COBUILD dictionary, as well as feeding modern technological tools, such as machine translation (more on this in Chapter 7).

2.2.4 How small can variants get?

We are aware that there is variation at different levels of structures. We know the debate surrounding whether there are true variants beyond the realm of phonology but also, regardless of true variants, that variation in language use can be observed at all structural levels. Approaching things from the opposite perspective, a question that begs to be asked is: how small do variants get? It might be useful here to consider the work on sound symbolism that "conventionalizes resemblance to things in the natural world" (Eckert 2019: 262). An experiment that was conducted as early as the 1920s that presented speakers with nonsense words showed that certain vowels such as [a] "say AH" evoked the sense of a greater volume (Sapir 1929). Sapir (1929) explained that there was kinaesthetic resemblance between the tongue position and larger resonance cavity involved in producing [a] and the notion of a larger reference. Work by D'onofrio (2014) on the nature of nonsense words showed that phonetic features mattered in how participants matched the nonsense word with a reference shape. Phonetic features here include whether consonants were voiced (for instance, contrast [b] and [p], and you will notice that your vocal chords do not vibrate with [p], as the consonant is voiceless), place of articulation (where in your oral tract is there a closure or almost a closure?), and even backness of vowel (horizontal position of tongue involved in producing vowel). It is unsurprising, then, that acoustic features themselves can be used for the purpose of sociolinguistic variation. For example, Pratt (2020) establishes that tech students at an art-focused high school in the San Francisco Bay Area showed significant backing of the LOT vowel and word initial /l/, which seems to suggest that a retracted jaw setting is associated with perceptions of being tough and ready for manual labour. Separately, a study on Baba Malay, an endangered contact language spoken in Singapore and Malaysia, demonstrated how vowel frontness could be associated with the notion of refinedness. The language has refined forms of words that are usually encoded with [ɛ] (the vowel in AIR). A matched guise perception task showed that listeners were more likely to rate guises or presented forms as being more refined when they were perceived to be produced further front in the oral cavity, associating in effect the smaller articulatory space created by fronting a vowel with the notion of something more delicate and refined (Lee 2020). What these studies go to show is that variation can take place on a very minute scale!

The matched guise task

It should be clear by now that there are multiple methods of approaching variationist sociolinguistics and that while observing speech production is one of the primary approaches, studying speech perception is also highly useful. The matched guise task is arguably one of the most useful tools in studying speech perception.

The matched guise task was conceived by Canadian linguists Wallace Lambert and colleagues in the 1960s to evaluate attitudes of bilingual French Canadian towards French as well as English in Montreal. In the **matched guise** task, listeners are asked to listen to audio clips and rate the guises they hear on various character traits, which can run the gamut from socioeconomic success to sociability, not knowing that they were listening to the same speaker or speakers perform both guises.

> Lambert et al. (1960) showed that Anglophone participants rated English guises more favourably than the French ones but that Francophone participants also rated English guises more favourably than the French ones, plausibly cognizant of the socioeconomic circumstances experienced in Montreal at that time that favoured English speakers.
>
> The matched guise task is a powerful way of understanding perception, as self-reports regarding linguistic attitudes can often be unreliable, and is still used to a great extent in current sociolinguistics.

2.3 Traditional dimensions of variation

The multiple examples in the previous sections show that language use in terms of production and perception can vary due to major sociological factors such as class, gender, ethnicity, and age. Of course, language use can vary due to other sorts of factors such as affiliation and group membership as well, but for now, let us begin by focusing on the categories that have formed the major basis of research in the most traditional of sociolinguistic variationist studies.

2.3.1 Social class

Social class is central to traditional work in sociolinguistics. **Social class** as a construct can be operationalised through measures such as looking at the type of properties that one's family owns, the level of one's income, and the types of jobs that one engages in, as well as possibly one's educational level, or by looking at a combination of these factors (and to a certain extent, the way one is perceived in relation to these social factors).

It is clear that class differences can result in language variation. In the fictionalised world of George Bernard Shaw's play *Pygmalion* (a perhaps more popular version is the 1964 movie *My Fair Lady*), we see Henry Higgins, a linguist, attempt to coach Eliza Doolitle, a flower girl from the lower class, so that her speech and behaviour would pass her off as someone belonging to the upper class. While we know that teaching "proper" speech is certainly not the concern of any linguist, the story emphasises speech as highly reflective of social class. It is indeed true that social stratification occurs in just about any society, and with that, a myriad of possibilities for language variation to take place. For instance, in Labov's New York departmental store study (mentioned in Chapter 1), we learned that the employees at three different stores reflecting three different social classes (working, middle, and upper) had different realisations of /r/. Those serving customers from the higher class were most likely to fully pronounce /r/, those serving customers from the working class were more likely to drop /r/, and those catering to customers in the middle class were somewhere in between both ends of that scale. Not surprisingly, rhoticity in this study was highly linked to socioeconomic class. On a different yet related topic of aspirations, a PhD dissertation on the use of Beijing Mandarin by Zhao (2017) showed that four specific linguistic variables (neutral tone, classifier omission, intensifier *te*, and word-final rhotacisation) were used to "convey casualness" in Beijing Mandarin, where speakers were more likely to use them in informal scenarios such as with friends where they will not be perceived critically, compared to more formal scenarios (such as interviews or a work environment) where they use more standard Mandarin, given that their language use might come under greater scrutiny. These speakers were therefore style-shifting and avoiding these variables to appear more prestigious (in line with their aspirations) in more formal settings, as compared to informal settings where they highlight a prestige more associated with the local identity.

When language use goes beyond social class and the different types of prestige

While it is clear that social class plays a huge role in language variation, it is obvious that people's choices are not always constrained by social class. For example, one might expect everyone to aspire towards the speech of the middle or upper classes, but that is certainly not the case. If that was the case, and if a particular sort of speech could be learnt, then the world would certainly become very boring! Instead, we see that there are always a multitude of factors at play. For example, non-standard languages or dialects are often linked to the notion of covert prestige. Covert prestige as a notion came about when Labov, in his seminal study of variation in New York, noticed that speakers would still continue to use a nonstandard dialect despite there being clearly a less inferior choice that might be available to them (1966). These nonstandard varieties are often reflective of various types of group identities. For example, Hawai'i Creole English, also known as Pidgin to its speakers, is emblematic of the speakers' identities as Hawai'i locals despite the fact that it was once outright discriminated against in favour of Standard English (Yokota 2008). It is the language that many in Hawai'i grow up with as a first language and is largely used among friends and family. As of 2015, the language became recognised as an official language of Hawai'i (Chan Laddaran 2015). Standard varieties, on the other hand, are usually associated with overt prestige and indicative of higher socioeconomic standing (Trudgill 1972). In a separate study carried out on English speakers in Norwich, Trudgill (1972) further expanded on Labov's findings. He showed additionally that the male speakers in his study favoured nonstandard working-class varieties, as they conferred more solidarity, while female speakers valued sounding more standard and hence sounding like they were of a higher status.

2.3.2 Sex and gender

So, what does gender have to do with it all? We know very broadly that men and women speak differently, but we also know that gender rather than biological sex may affect language use (Labov 2001).

Traditional sociolinguistics tells us that female speakers are more likely to use standard and overtly prestigious forms than male speakers, particularly so in stable situations when it is clear which forms are used in what ways (Labov 2001). We see such a situation pan out with the female speakers in Trudgill's (1972) work, introduced in the previous section. In fact, we can more widely consider that alternation of [n] and [ŋ] (think IN and ING) in unstressed syllables in English. You could say "eating" or "eatin", and it would most probably be apparent to you that the former sounds more standard. Labov (2001) broadly surveyed what he and others had uncovered in various English-speaking locales within the United States, England, Australia, and the British Isles and surmised that female speakers were more likely to use the prestige ING variant. However, this should be thought of as a broad tendency, because women of the lowest social group in Labov's Philadelphia data, for example, showed the use of as many stigmatised variants (including the IN form) as men. And even within a group delineated by sex, there can be further variation depending on the types of activities that the speakers engage in. For example, ethnographic work at an all-girl's high school in New Zealand showed that how the girls spoke depended on whether the groups they participated in ate lunch in the common room or otherwise (Drager 2009) (see section on community of practice for more).

Broadly, it might almost sound like females are conservative in their speech patterns. And yet, having said all that, females are also known to be particularly innovative when it comes to new variants speakers themselves may not be conscious of. For example, the use of syllabic /m/ (the M sound in "mer") in place of syllabic /ŋ/ (the NG sound in ING) in Hong Kong Cantonese was first initiated by women in the 30–40 age range before teenage males took on the change (Bauer 1982). A word such as [ŋ mɐn] (sounding like NG MAHN) for 'five dollars' would be pronounced as [m mɐn] (M MAHN) in the more novel way. Similarly, in Seoul Korean, women were leading a change in raising /o/ (OH) to [u] (sounds like U as in "blue") in non-initial unstressed syllables concentrated in grammatical morphemes (meaningful parts of a word that contribute to grammar) (Chae 1995). So, instead of saying [mwərako] (sounding like: MWUHRAKO) for 'what did you say' or 'what did you mean', a woman leading the change might say [mwəraku] (MWUHRAKU) instead.

When do linguists use // and when do they use []?

What, then, is the difference between language sounds that appear in square brackets [] and those that appear in forward slashes //? Simply, the square brackets [] indicates a phonetic transcription (focused mostly on how things are actually pronounced), while things that appear in slashes // indicate a phonemic transcription that is more concerned with significant sounds that have the ability to change the meaning of the word. Therefore, [n] and [ŋ] are two ways of saying /ŋ/ in English, as with our earlier examples "eating" and "eatin".

Beyond biological sex, then, the importance of gender cannot be underestimated. A study conducted on online webboards in Thailand showed that *kathoey* (transgender women) and women were using epicene (gender-neutral) pronouns most of the time but also that *kathoey* were using significantly more feminine pronouns on the webboard for the trans community than women who were posting on webboards that cater to women (Saisuwan 2015). Therefore, it is not possible to simply talk about linguistic variation based on binary sex but to take a more inclusive perspective that also considers gender identity.

2.3.3 Ethnicity

Ethnicity is yet another large social category whose effects on language and linguistic variation cannot be taken lightly. Broadly speaking, **ethnicity** can be construed as a group whose membership relies on the perception that group members share particular attributes, such as shared ancestry, cultural practices, or even a common language. Ethnicity is by no means a straightforward construct, negotiated as it is between self-identification as well as the perception of others (Fought 2011). Take, for instance, an undergraduate in Singapore whose identity card stipulates that he is Malay and who is assumed by most who see and interact with him to be Malay (not least because he speaks the Malay language) but who says he is Jawi Peranakan (descendants of a locally born group in the Malay Archipelago, with mixed Indian and Malay ancestry as well as mixed Arab and Malay ancestry, whose history of intermarriages predates the 20th century). The attributes that are perceived to be shared by the group include not just ancestry but also religion (being Muslim), cuisine (influenced heavily by southern Indian cuisine), and fashion. Notably, some of these ways of being may also be associated with other ethnic identities, for example, with most Malays being Muslim. Ethnicity is, then, a complex shared identity but, significantly for sociolinguistics, one that has consequences for linguistic practices. It is not surprising, for example, that simply by speaking in a certain way, one can possibly pass oneself off as a group member of a particular ethnicity (Bucholtz 1995).

Ethnicity has a whole host of implications for gender, but we can consider the most obvious ones. Most perceptibly, there might be sociolinguistic features associated with particular ethnic groups. For example, in a study on Malaysian English that surveyed undergraduates, it was shown that the Tamil-speaking Indian participants completely replaced fricative /θ/ (think TH) with [t] in the final and initial positions of words, plausibly because /θ/ does not occur in Tamil and /f/ is a marginal, rarely used consonant in Tamil, as compared to other speakers such as the Malays, who were replacing the final fricative with [f], which sounds more phonetically similar to [θ] (both being fricatives, meaning that they are produced by forcing air out through a narrow passage in the mouth) (Phoon, Abdullah & Maclagen 2013). Another way in which language engages or disengages from ethnicity is when there are conflicting pressures to sound more standard as compared to sounding more "authentic". Fordham and Ogbu (1986) discuss how African American students may do poorly at school, partly because they are discouraged from acting White, and that those who sound overly standard may also be perceived negatively, even though sounding more standard is often required in middle-class jobs, for example.

This brings us to the last point on this list, which does not claim to be an exhaustive, as ethnicity is a complicated, multifaceted issue. Sounding "ethnic" also has other sorts of repercussions for class, as in the previous instance, and other types of social categories such as gender (Fought 2011). For example, Meyerhoff (2004) examines attitudes towards Pidgin speakers in Hawai'i and makes comparisons with Bislama, showing that that female speakers of creoles are often evaluated more negatively than male speakers.

2.3.4 Age

The study of age is yet another important consideration in variationist sociolinguistics. We know that speech features are not constant over one's lifetime. For example, Queen Elizabeth II's pronunciation was said to have changed throughout her lifetime, so that her Received Pronunciation vowels became more influenced by standard southern British accent of the 1980s, typically associated with speakers who are younger and lower on the social hierarchy (Harrington, Palethorpe & Watson 2000). In general, the approach of following language change at different points in times, through history, in some cases, is known as the **real-time** approach. Such an approach contrasts with the notion of an **apparent time** approach, which focuses on comparing the patterns of different age groups, given that it is often difficult to go far back in time with linguistic data if the data has not been collected yet. If differences exist between younger and older speakers, and if these differences do not come about because of naturally being in that particular age group in what is known as **age-grading** (for example, adults being more conservative in their use of sociolinguistic features due to workplace pressures) (Eckert 1997), then we assume that there is language change in progress in that particular community.

As an example of the effect of age on sociolinguistic variation, we can return to the study on Tamil speakers of English in Singapore (highlighted earlier). Using a range of production tasks, the production of prevocalic /r/ in Singapore English is analysed across two groups that vary in ages. While home language, phonological environment, and cultural context also played a part (with these non-approximant/r/s being a means of indexing Indianness), older speakers were found to use more tapped /r/s than younger speakers as a whole (Starr & Balasubramaniam 2019).

2.3.5 Social networks

Yet another crucial concept in variationist sociolinguistics is the notion of social networks. The **social network** can be thought of as a "boundless web of ties" that connects people to one another (Milroy & Milroy 1992: 1). In their ground-breaking study, Milroy and Milroy quantified whether a network tie was dense by considering membership in a local group, having ties with at least two other households in the same neighbourhood, sharing a workplace with two or more individuals from the neighbourhood, sharing the workplace with same-sex individuals from the same neighbourhood, and being involved in voluntary activities from the same workplace (1978). What they found was that those with a high network strength score, meaning that they were fully immersed in their local community, used more local forms associated with that place (Milroy & Milroy 1978).

Friend of a friend

The 'friend of a friend' method was used in the Belfast study, which means that participants were contacted to participate in the experiment by their friends and acquaintances. Through such a method, the researcher is not a complete outsider, which may have repercussions what on what is observed. Participants are also less likely to say no to the researcher if they are introduced by an intermediary they know (Milroy & Gordon 2003). Networks themselves can also become apparent, if this is an important notion in the study. Of course, note that researchers do have to obtain consent for the study and abide by research ethics.

Research ethics

With the experimental nature of variationist sociolinguistics, it is necessary to broach the topic of ethics.

It is of utmost importance that participants in any experiment give their informed consent, meaning that they understand what their participation entails and are comfortable with taking part in the study. Informed consent can come in the form of a signed document or a recorded statement. While sociolinguistic studies may not have the capacity to cause potential physical harm, they have the ability of harming reputations, for example, if someone says something that is identifiable to them and if what they say is ever held against them for any reason. As such, it is important in many instances to provide anonymity, unless the participants outright ask to not be anonymous (which can be the case in language documentation data; see the chapter on language documentation). Regarding ethics, Labov (1982) has also stated the importance of correcting errors when one's research is invalidated by data that emerges, as well as by using the knowledge based on data collected from a community of speakers to benefit said community, when the need arises.

Note that within the short constraints of an introductory textbook, I acknowledge that this short passage is woefully insufficient. If you ever do conduct experimental study, please do consult your university's ethics review board to ensure you fully understand the implications of your study.

In any case, the consequences of not observing ethical responsibilities can have major consequences. As a quick exercise, look up the Stanford prison experiment and find out what went wrong and what the consequences were in this psychology experiment.

Today, it has become easier to conceptualise the network, with the advent of digital social networks such as Facebook and LinkedIn. The notion of the network continues to be useful in sociolinguistics and in variationist sociolinguistics, as in other subfields, such as in the study of language maintenance (see Chapter 5 on language endangerment for more).

2.3.6 Speech community versus community of practice

It should be clear from the previous subsections that there really are two different types of spheres of interaction that we are looking at. The first type of interaction sphere is that of the more traditional notion of the speech community. I use the term "traditional" because it goes as far back as with the work of Gauchat, who was in actuality looking at the speech community of Charmey, a French-speaking village in Switzerland. The **speech community** in general can be conceived as a group of people who regularly and frequently interact by means of a shared verbal system and societal norms (Gumperz 1968). The speech community can refer to spheres of relatively different sizes. It can refer to speakers of a variety of language, a dialect, the language of a neighbourhood, a town, or even a city, as in the work of Labov (1966). The Mandarin speakers in Malaysia can be a speech community, Baba Malay speakers can be a speech community; so can the speakers of Gurindji Kriol—you get the drift.

Then we have second sphere of interaction, the **community of practice**, which refers to a group of people who participate in a sustained, common endeavour (Eckert 2006). This is a more micro setting than the speech community, which is important for recognising how speakers engage locally in ways that are meaningful for language. For example, Drager (2009) discusses the differences in speech of girls who ate lunch in the common room versus those who did not at a high school in New Zealand. Pratt (2020) showed that students in the technical theatre department of an arts-focused high school in the San Francisco Bay Area produced higher and more rounded variants of the LOT vowel and more velarised productions of /l/ than their non-tech peers. Baran (2014) showed that for Mandarin-speaking students in a Taipei high school, a de-retroflection of [ʂ] (sounds like S in English but produced with the tip of the tongue curled up towards the hard palate of the mouth; a de-retroflection therefore means the loss of tongue-curling) and labial glide deletion (loss of [w] before [wɔ]) took place based on the *banji* 'class' of the students who shared the same curriculum, schedule, and classrooms for three years.

Given what you understand of these concepts, then, what are some speech communities that you can identify, and what are some communities of practice you think you might be able to identify?

Ethnography in sociolinguistics

A lot of community of practice work in variationist sociolinguistics centres around schools, where ethnographic work is made possible. Ethnographic work itself doesn't have to be of a school—it can be of a sports club, a group of people at a shared workplace, a cultural association, and so on. It really is an approach where the researchers have learnt to orient themselves towards the shared norms, culture, and interests of the community they are observing. You might ask why ethnography is important. Remember that researchers aren't just researchers but participants within their own communities with their own values they subscribe to, which can sometimes lead to them being less sensitive to what is happening in other communities. It often requires long-term participation for the ethnographic approach to yield meaningful observations regarding how language works in the community—long term not least because it takes a while before the researcher is no longer simply an outsider but becomes somewhat accepted within the community (remember the Observer's Paradox?).

2.4 What is register and style?

At the beginning of the book, one of the things we talked about was how we speak differently in different circumstances or when particular domains or interlocutors call for different ways of speaking. You most likely speak in what we call a more formal "register" when you are giving a presentation as part of your undergraduate course. You use perhaps a different informal register when you are talking with your friends. You certainly would not be using 'rizz' (if you were speaking in

2022 or 2023) in your undergraduate presentation unless you were presenting about 'rizz', and you wouldn't be peppering that same presentation with 'oh my gosh!' In Javanese, speakers can vary between three registers—*ngko* 'informal', *madya* 'intermediate formality', and *krama* 'formal'. The *ngoko* level of speech is thought to be the most non-polite and used only with people one is familiar with; *krama* is the most polite level and used towards those who command the most respect, whereas *madya* is an intermediate level between the two. For example, 'to tell or ask someone to do something' is *akon* in *ngoko*, *kèn* in *madya*, and *kèngkèn* or *purèh* in *krama* (Poedjosoedarmo 1968). Registers can also go beyond the formal and informal. For example, in Malay, one might use *isteri* for 'wife' if they were trying to sound more *halus* 'refined', whereas *bini* would be the *kasar* 'coarse' version of the word.

Register and style are somewhat used interchangeably, but **register** has been more associated with a set of vocabulary used in a particular situation, whereas **styles** can vary based on grammar as well. For example, phonological variation occurs when one says 'walkin'' instead of 'walking'. Style can differ from register in that it represents a personal stance on an issue. For example, a speaker can be in a formal context but use 'oh my gosh', or 'gonna' instead of 'going to', because they are creating a specific sort of social image. Often, such a style is also associated with other ways in which speakers present themselves. Language is just one of the many tools, and fashion can be another. In the 1980s, it became apparent that "new wavers" at a Palo Alto high school in California were wearing mostly dark clothes and using dark eye make-up, whereas "preppy" girls were wearing pastels and using either light or no eye make-up (Eckert 2000).

Of course, speakers can style-shift based on situation as well. One can certainly switch stances and personas when speaking, depending on the situation, for example, switching to a more colloquial speech when among local friends versus foreign friends. What other situations can you think about in which you style-shift?

Hypercorrection

Now that we have covered the notions of more formal versus informal registers and talked about more standard versus more

> colloquial speech, it would make sense to talk about the phenomenon of hypercorrection. **Hypercorrection** comes about when someone is aspiring towards a more formal, more standard way of speaking but ends up making a mistake instead, often through false analogy or the overapplication of a rule. For instance, "octopi" is used by some as the plural form of "octopus", under the impression that Latin-derived words should have the Latin ending -*i* in English, even though "octopus" is in actuality derived from Greek and not Latin. Likewise, some people would say "He called you and I" instead of "he called you and me" because they are overapplying the rule that "You and I" is the correct form in subject position (before the verb) to the object position (after the verb). Look out for hypercorrection in your own speech or the speech of people around you—it might be more common than you think it is!

2.4.1 What is accommodation theory and audience design?

Finally, and still related to styles and style-shifting, are the notions of accommodation theory and audience design. **Accommodation theory** has it that speakers either diverge or converge with (accommodate) their interlocutors based on social and psychological motivations. Speakers can be more unlike or alike the people they are speaking with, based on what they want out of the conversation, whether they want to be liked by their interlocutor or if they dislike the person, whether one person has more power than the other or if they want to establish dominance over the other, and so on and so forth. There are many reasons we might choose to sound more like whom we are conversing with or otherwise (Giles, Coupland & Coupland 1991). **Audience design**, inspired by work on accommodation theory, draws on the idea that style-shifting happens to accommodate the audience or otherwise. Speakers can vary their speech towards that of their audience to express solidarity with them; likewise they can vary their speech if they are trying to maintain distance from their audience. The notion that speakers adjust the way they speak according to their audience came about in research that showed how newsreaders from two different stations (one which attracted audiences with higher socioeconomic statuses and another which attracted audiences with lower socioeconomic statuses) varied in their use of sociolinguistic variables even though they were engaged in the same activity of broadcasting the news and that some of these newsreaders were essentially the same person engaged by both stations. The only explanation, then, for why the newsreaders' speech varied across both stations is to be found in how they were accommodating towards their audience (Bell 1984).

Over the next couple of days, observe how you speak, towards whom is it that you accommodate your speech, and why you think those are the people towards whom you are accommodating. Who are the people you are diverging your speech from, and why are you diverging your speech away from them? The study of sociolinguistics may seem complex, but it really is found in your everyday life, and variation is so ingrained in you that perhaps you do it reflexively and instinctively without thinking too much about it.

References

Baran, Dominika. 2014. Linguistic practice and identity work: Variation in Taiwan Mandarin at a Taipei County high school. *Journal of Sociolinguistics* 18(1). 32–59. https://doi.org/10.1111/josl.12068.

Bauer, Robert S. 1982. Lexical diffusion in Hong Kong Cantonese: "Five" leads the way. *Annual Meeting of the Berkeley Linguistics Society*, 550–561. https://doi.org/10.3765/bls.v8i0.2037.

Bell, Allan. 1984. Language style as audience design. *Language in Society*. Cambridge University Press 13(2). 145–204.

Bucholtz, Mary. 1995. From Mulatta to Mestiza: Passing and the linguistic reshaping of ethnic identity. In Kira Hall & Mary Bucholtz (eds.), *Gender Articulated: Language and the Socially Constructed Self*, 351–373. New York: Routledge.

Chae, Seo-Yeong. 1995. *External Constraints on Sound Change: The Raising of /o/ in Seoul Korean*. Philadelphia: University of Pennsylvania PhD dissertation.

Chan Laddaran, Bu Kerry. 2015. Pidgin English now an official language of Hawaii. *CNN*. www.cnn.com/2015/11/12/living/pidgin-english-hawaii/index.html. (29 August, 2023).

Cheshire, Jenny. 2005. Syntactic variation and beyond: Gender and social class variation in the use of discourse-new markers. *Journal of Sociolinguistics* 9(4). 479–508. https://doi.org/10.1111/j.1360-6441.2005.00303.x.

Cheshire, Jenny & Ann Williams. 2002. Information structure in male and female adolescent talk. *Journal of English Linguistics*. SAGE Publications Inc 30(2). 217–238. https://doi.org/10.1177/007242030002008.

D'Onofrio, Annette. 2014. Phonetic detail and dimensionality in sound-shape correspondences: Refining the Bouba-Kiki paradigm. *Language and Speech*. SAGE Publications Ltd 57(3). 367–393. https://doi.org/10.1177/0023830913507694.

Drager, Katie. 2009. *A Sociophonetic Ethnography of Selwyn Girls' High*. University of Canterbury. Languages, Cultures and Linguistics. http://hdl.handle.net/10092/4185. (6 December, 2023).

Eckert, Penelope. 1997. Age as a sociolinguistic variable. In Florian Coulmas (ed.), *The Handbook of Sociolinguistics*, 151–167. Oxford: Blackwell.

Eckert, Penelope. 2000. *Linguistic Variation as Social Practice*. Oxford: Blackwell.

Eckert, Penelope. 2006. Community of practice. In Keith Brown (ed.), *Encyclopedia of Language and Linguistics*, 683–685. 2nd edition. Amsterdam: Elsevier.

Eckert, Penelope. 2019. The limits of meaning: Social indexicality, variation, and the cline of interiority. *Language* 95(4). 751–776.

Fordham, Signithia & John U. Ogbu. 1986. Black students' school success: Coping with the "burden of acting White". *The Urban Review*. Germany: Springer 18(3). 176–206. https://doi.org/10.1007/BF01112192.

Fought, Carmen. 2011. Language and ethnicity. In Rajend Mesthrie (ed.), *The Cambridge Handbook of Sociolinguistics* (Cambridge Handbooks in Language and Linguistics), 238–258. Cambridge: Cambridge University Press. https://doi.org/10.1017/CBO9780511997068.019.

Giles, Howard, Justine Coupland & Nikolas Coupland (eds.). 1991. *Contexts of Accomodation*. Cambridge: Cambridge University Press.

Gonzales, Wilkinson Daniel Wong. 2023. Spread, stability, and sociolinguistic variation in multilingual practices: The case of Lánnang-uè and its derivational morphology. *International Journal of Multilingualism*. Routledge 21(3). 1547–1574. https://doi.org/10.1080/14790718.2023.2199998.

Gumperz, John. 1968. The speech community. In *International Encyclopedia of the Social Sciences*, 381–386. New York: Macmillan.

Harrington, Jonathan, Sallyanne Palethorpe & Catherine I. Watson. 2000. Does the queen speak the queen's English? *Nature* 408. 927–928.

Labov, William. 1963. The social motivation of a sound change. *Word* 18. 1–42.

Labov, William. 1966. *The Social Stratification of English in New York City*. Washington, DC: Center for Applied Linguistics.
Labov, William. 1972a. The social motivation of a sound change. In William Labov (ed.), *Sociolinguistic Patterns*, 1–42. Philadelphia: University of Pennsylvania Press.
Labov, William. 1972b. *Sociolinguistic Patterns* (Sociolinguistic Patterns). Philadelphia: University of Pennsylvania Press.
Labov, William. 1982. Objectivity and commitment in linguistic science. *Language in Society* 11. 165–201.
Labov, William. 1984. Field methods of the project on linguistic change. In John Baugh & Joel Sherzer (eds.), *Language in Use: Readings in Sociolinguistics*, 28–53. Englewood Cliffs: Prentice-Hall, Inc.
Labov, William. 2001. *Principles of Linguistic Change: Social Factors*. Malden/Oxford: Blackwell Publishers.
Lambert, Wallace E., Richard Hodgson, Robert C. Gardner & Samuel Fillenbaum. 1960. Evaluational reactions to spoken languages. *Journal of Abnormal and Social Psychology* 60(1). 44–51.
Lee, Nala H. 2020. Style variation in the second formant: What does it mean to be "refined" in Baba Malay? *Language Ecology*. John Benjamins 4(1). 115–130. https://doi.org/10.1075/le.00012.lee.
Meyerhoff, Miriam. 2004. Attitudes to gender and creoles: A case study on mokes and titas. *Te Reo* 47. 63–82.
Milroy, James & Lesley Milroy. 1978. Belfast: Change and variation in an urban vernacular. In Peter Trudgill (ed.), *Sociolinguistic Patterns in British English*, 19–36. London: Edward Arnold.
Milroy, Lesley & Matthew Gordon. 2003. *Sociolinguistics: Methods and Interpretation*. Oxford: Blackwell.
Milroy, Lesley & James Milroy. 1992. Social network and social class: Towards an integrated sociolinguistic model. *Language in Society* 21. 1–26.
Phoon, Hooi San, Christina Abdullah & Margaret Maclagen. 2013. The consonant realizations of Malay-, Chinese- and Indian-influenced Malaysian English. *Australian Journal of Linguistics* 33(1). 3–30.
Pillai, Stefanie. 2015. Rhoticity in Malaysian English: The emergence of a new norm? In Ulrike Gut, Robert Fuchs & Eva-Maria Wunder (eds.), *Universal or Diverse Paths to English Phonology*, 23–40. Berlin: Walter de Gruyter.
Poedjosoedarmo, Soepomo. 1968. Javanese speech levels. *Indonesia* 6. 54–81.
Pratt, Teresa. 2020. Embodying "tech": Articulatory setting, phonetic variation, and social meaning. *Journal of Sociolinguistics* 24(3). 328–349. https://doi.org/10.1111/josl.12369.

Saisuwan, Pavadee. 2015. Kathoey and the linguistic construction of gender identity in Thailand. In Erez Levon & Ronald Beline Mendes (eds.), *Language, Sexuality, and Power: Studies in Intersectional Sociolinguistics*, 189–214. Oxford University Press. https://doi.org/10.1093/acprof:oso/9780190210366.003.0010.

Sankoff, David & Pierrette Thibault. 1981. Weak complementarity: Tense and aspect in Montreal French. In Brenda B. Johns & David R. Strang (eds.), *Syntactic Change*, 205–216. Ann Arbor: Department of Linguistics, University of Michigan.

Sapir, Edward. 1929. A study in phonetic symbolism. *Journal of Experimental Psychology*. US: Psychological Review Company 12(3). 225–239. https://doi.org/10.1037/h0070931.

Starr, Rebecca Lurie & Brinda Balasubramaniam. 2019. Variation and change in English /r/ among Tamil Indian Singaporeans. *World Englishes* 38(4). 630–643. https://doi.org/10.1111/weng.12357.

Tagliamonte, Sali A. (ed.). 2006. The sociolinguistic interview. In *Analysing Sociolinguistic Variation* (Key Topics in Sociolinguistics), 37–76. Cambridge: Cambridge University Press. https://doi.org/10.1017/CBO9780511801624.005.

Tan, Ying-Ying. 2012. To r or not to r: Social correlates of /ɹ/ in Singapore English. *International Journal of the Sociology of Language*. De Gruyter Mouton 2012(218). 1–24. https://doi.org/10.1515/ijsl-2012-0057.

Trudgill, Peter. 1972. Sex, covert prestige and linguistic change in the urban British English of Norwich. *Language in Society* 1(2). 179–195.

Yokota, Thomas. 2008. The "Pidgin problem": Attitudes about Hawai'i Creole. *Educational Perspectives* 31(1–2). 22–29.

Zhao, Hui. 2017. *Language Variation and Social Identity in Beijing*. London: Queen Mary University of London PhD dissertation.

Chapter 3

Multilingualism

3.1 What is multilingualism and bilingualism?

Multilingualism is characterised by the ability of individuals or society to communicate effectively in more than one language. **Bilingualism** is commonly used to describe speakers who can use two languages effectively. Note that the terms 'trilingual', 'quadrilingual', and 'quintilingual' also exist but are less often used as we go up the ladder in terms of how many languages one can speak. Another thing that should become clear is how important the notion of being able to effectively communicate in all these other languages is in these definitions. You wouldn't label yourself as being 'bilingual' in Japanese, for example, if your language competence was limited to the Japanese words for items on a sushi conveyor belt. It is clearly a whole different matter to understand and be understood by Japanese people when communicating in their language. Linguists understand that there is some level of competence required for one to be considered bilingual or multilingual. François Grosjean, for example, defined bilingualism as the use of two (or more) languages in one's everyday life but not necessarily knowing these languages equally well and optimally (1984). Leonard Bloomfield, on the other hand, stated that one had to have native-like control of two or more languages to be considered bilingual (1933). The truth of the matter is that the level of proficiency required for one to be considered bilingual or multilingual remains a matter of debate. Tangentially, it might also be interesting to consider how some of these linguists were using 'bilingual' as a stand-in for 'multilingual'. These concepts are rather similar in terms of the approaches that linguists can take with them and how they are described. With that in mind, this chapter will use 'multilingualism' as a general term unless specifically citing studies that deal strictly with bilingualism.

Before we delve into it any further, it is perhaps important to state how common and unexotic multilingualism actually is. That multilingualism is rare is a myth perpetuated in heavily monolingual Western-centric countries that may only associate the phenomenon with other specific Western countries as an exception, such as Canada, Switzerland, and Belgium (Grosjean 1997). As introduced in Chapter 1, multilingualism has long been the norm in many parts of the world. For instance, the ancient Mediterranean world was known to have been multilingual since many centuries BCE. In fact, it has been noted that the more extensively empires developed, the more linguistically diverse they became (as with the Assyrians, Babylonians, and Persians) (Jonker, Berlejung & Cornelius 2021). It was only much later that the "one language/one culture/one nation" paradigm emerged (Pujolar 2007), which put an end to the notion that multilingualism was normal. This was and is the language situation in some large Western nation states. Over 75 percent of the 127 million people surveyed in a 2021 population census of the United States stated that they spoke only English, as compared to India, where people are highly multilingual and where between 200 and 700 languages from at least four language families are spoken across the populace (Pattanayak 1990). While clearly not all places are like India, the reality is that most places in the world have more multilinguals than monolinguals and that they are found across different classes and age groups, having attained their languages at different stages in their lives (Grosjean 1997). Given that much sociolinguistics research comes out of the Western tradition, this has skewed how multilingualism is (not) represented. Take **variationist sociolinguistics**, for example. It is recognised that most of the work in this tradition comes from a monolingual English perspective. It is therefore enriching and even necessary to consider what we can possibly learn about language and society through the perspective of multilingualism. We do so in the chapter by looking at multilingualism at the level of society and the individual.

3.2 How does society juggle more than one language?

3.2.1 Diglossia

The term '**diglossia**' was popularised by sociolinguist Charles A. Ferguson to describe a specific stable sort of relationship between two varieties of the same language (1959). We have different languages or language varieties being used for what we deem H (high) versus L (low) functions, H here referring to the more formal sorts of functions and domains and L referring to the more informal ones. The H variety would be a standard sort of variety that is learned formally in school and used in official settings such as in parliament or courts. The L variety, on the other hand, would be the H language's non-standard, unofficial, unwritten counterpart that is used in the community. This would be a language that is often thought of as being corrupt but used as the main language at home. The relationship between Standard Singapore English and Colloquial Singapore English (known as Singlish) can be thought of as being diglossic in that way—Singlish is often thought of as being a corrupt, broken version of Standard Singapore English and is not officially endorsed in schools and for formal purposes as the standard variety is, yet it is acquired at home and used informally by most Singaporeans. At this point, you might be thinking, how, then, is diglossia related to multilingualism?

As is the case, in a later iteration, diglossia was expanded to deal with situations of bilingualism by Joshua A. Fishman so that the languages in a diglossic relationship do not necessarily have to be genetically related (1967). Likewise, diglossia in the bilingual situation refers to when there is a dichotomous relationship between an L language and a H language. An example that Fishman brings up is the pre-war Eastern European Jewish male, who would use Yiddish (a Germanic language) as the L language and Hebrew (a Semitic language) as the H language, although he also noted that post-war, they would have adopted a third Western language to communicate with other groups (mostly English).

Interestingly, you might find in reality that a lot of diglossic relationships are more nuanced than straightforward. According to the narrower version of diglossia that looks at the relationship between genetically related languages, Haitian Creole would function as the L language, while French would function as the H language, given the French language's overt sort of prestige and its use as the language of most schools. However, Haitian Creole and French are both recognised as official languages in Haiti. Complicating matters further, it is estimated that around 90 percent of Haitians speak only Haitian Creole (Hebblethwaite 2021). The same goes for diglossia between unrelated languages.

> ## Diglossia where you live
>
> Think about it. Do you live in a multilingual society, and would you describe the language situation as being diglossic? Can you clearly identify what the H language is and what the L language is? Why or why not? Is the L language only ever used for L purposes, and likewise, is the H language only ever used for H purposes?

3.2.2 Functions and domains of use

With **diglossia**, we are traditionally concerned with a pair of language varieties or languages. Given a multilingual setting, who speaks what language to whom and when becomes an interesting question (Fishman 1965). In view of this, **domains of language use** can be thought of as particular groupings of sociological settings and institutional contexts, alongside participants (Fishman 1965: 19). The five traditional domains that were first identified by Fishman (1972) are family, friendship, religion, education, and employment. Some of these domains are associated with some level of informality and hence viewed as L sorts of domains, such as family and friendship, while others are thought of as being a lot more formal, such as education and employment. Very clearly, in a multilingual environment, the language that we use in school with our teachers and at work with our employers may not be the very same language that is used at home with our family or with friends. For example, in India, the language that is used in school can be Hindi and English, alongside a state language, such as Punjabi in the state of Punjab, while other minority languages are spoken at home.

> ### The social media domain: H or L?
>
> It is notable that as society changes, domains evolve as well. For example, the online computer-mediated domain is an important one to consider, a sub-variety of which notably would be social media. Where you are from, what language do you use for social media? Do you consider it an H or L language? Why do you think an L or H language is used for this purpose?

The notion of domains is useful in particular when considering how the social contexts of languages can change and evolve to the extent that the language becomes endangered. In general, a language that becomes restricted to fewer domains is more likely to be less viable in the long run than a language that is not similarly restricted in use. We will broach this further in Chapter 5 when we consider the topic of language endangerment.

3.2.3 Ideologies of multilingualism and monolingualism

Moving away from functions and use for a bit, it becomes apparent that society has some pretty strong beliefs about multilingualism and monolingualism. Collectively, beliefs about language structure and language use that tell us something about the political and economic interests of people, groups, and nations that they belong to are known as **language ideologies** (Fuller 2018). These sorts of beliefs are also often seen in the explicit policies and legislations that governments enact (Fuller 2018) (see the following section).

3.2.3.1 One language, one nation

One prominent ideology is the **one language, one nation ideology**. In particular, the rise of nationalism has had repercussions on the way people think about language. Nationalism is an ideology characterised by people's identification with their nation and their loyalty towards it. It is the belief that the administrative boundaries of one's nation coincide with the use of a single language and that the use of a common language acts as somewhat of a unifying instrument. Such an ideology affects individuals' beliefs about what speakers in their countries should rightfully speak, for example, that Americans should speak English and that Indonesians should speak Bahasa Indonesia (Alisjahbana 1949), even though English was never indigenous to the United States and notwithstanding the fact that there are more than 700 languages spoken in Indonesia alone (Anderbeck 2015). The efforts to centre one's nation-building discourse around one language are often highly conscious and deliberate endeavours. For example, Bahasa Indonesia was deliberately sought as a national language as part of Indonesia's self-determining nationalistic movement in the wake of its history of colonisation by the Portuguese and the Spanish, to the Dutch, the British, and the Japanese (Harper 2013).

While the one language, one nation ideology may or may not be intended to have particular consequences beyond drawing together some sense of collective nationhood, it is often the case that such an ideology results in prejudice against other languages and speakers of other languages.

3.2.3.2 Hegemony

Linguistic hegemony comes about when pressure is put upon speakers of languages other than the chosen language of the nation to assimilate (Eriksen 1992). The notion here is that one language is superior to the others, and this can affect attitudes surrounding multilingualism and have a deleterious effect on other languages, and consequently on linguistic diversity. For example, a significant number of people in America believe that multilingualism is un-American (Kircher & Kutlu 2023; Fuller 2018). Such a view stems from a belief that it is more natural for a state to be monolingual than multilingual, and anyone not white, monocultural, and monolingual is immediately deemed non-American (Fuller 2013). Clearly, such an ideology puts an immense pressure on speakers of less dominant languages to assimilate, and this can threaten minority languages (Eriksen 1992) by making the transmission and learning of these minority languages less attractive and desirable (see Chapter 5 on language endangerment).

3.2.3.3 Language purity

Also associated with monolingual practices of one language, one nation and linguistic hegemony is the notion of **language purity**—that there is a language that is purer and therefore more worthy than its more corrupted varieties. In the case of Indonesia, where Bahasa Indonesia is seen as the unifying language of the nation, "'good and true' Indonesian has been promoted by means of institutes, publishing projects, the school system, television programs, and official exhortations" (Keane 2003: 518). Likewise, we see the *Académie Française* 'French Academy' as an institution that is highly involved in 'governing' how French should be spoken. Anglicisims, or the use of English terms that are borrowed into the language, are viewed as an "invasion", for example, and the Académie advocates inventing French **neologisms** and using these new terms instead of Anglicisms (Académie Française 2024). For instance, with the rise of eSports and competitive gaming entering mainstream media, government officials have been urged to not use borrowed terms such as "eSports" or "streamer" when discussing related issues, but to use 'proper' French terms to describe them such as *jeu video de competition* and *joueur-animateur en direct*, respectively, even if they are more verbose terms (BBC 2022).

3.2.3.4 Market language ideology

Beyond protecting one's national language, a different perspective is offered by the **market language ideology** (Dickinson 2010), where the goal is communication in which speakers use whatever linguistic resources they have. Such an ideology can be shared by speakers or outright institutionalised by policymakers, who value an ability to communicate beyond one's national borders for the purpose of participating in the global economy. As a case in point, Japan is known to be heavily monolingual but has stated that "global literacy" is one of its larger goals for its populace. English has become increasingly dominant as the language of commerce and business in Japan, to the extent that it was declared the official language of use for companies such as Uniqlo (Fujita-Round & Maher 2017).

3.2.3.5 Mother tongue ideology

What, then, of the home domain? How can ideology permeate the home domain? The **mother tongue ideology** appears to pertain to the home domain but in actual fact, it is one that affects individuals in very public ways and in official domains. It is the belief that individuals have one mother tongue, and one that may prioritise the use of this language for that particular individual over other languages in particular domains. For example, in Luxembourg, French and German are stipulated official languages of the workplace, while Luxembourgish is the home language or mother tongue that Luxembourg citizens are meant to use with each other on a more casual basis (Horner & Weber 2008). A huge issue, however, with any country that practices a mother tongue ideology is that it presents a homogenous view of the populace involved. This is the case in Luxembourg, as well as in Singapore, where students experience an English-based bilingual education system. In addition to learning English and learning through English as a medium of instruction, school-going children in Singapore are supposed to learn an additional 'mother tongue' that is meant to reflect the language of their homes—the Chinese learn Mandarin, the Malays learn the Malay language, and the Indians learn Tamil (Sim 2016). The home experience of the Chinese, regardless of whether their families speak Southern Min, Cantonese, Hakka, or Hainanese; the home experiences of those categorised to be Malays, including those who would originally define themselves as Javanese, Boyanese, Bugis, or Minangkabau; and of course the home experiences of a larger category of southern Indians are conflated into single categories within mainstream education.

3.2.4 Language planning and policies

What we have seen in the previous are instances of **language planning**. Language planning is thought of as a rather "authoritative allocation of resources to the attainment of language status and corpus goals" (Fishman 1987: 407). In this regard, language planning is often twofold: it encourages the use of specific languages, hence raising their statuses, while discouraging the use of others. **Corpus planning**, on the other hand, relates to the outright regulation, change, and often standardisation of a language itself in a rather prescriptive way.

Two viewpoints on language

Linguistic prescriptivism is the view that there are correct and wrong ways of using a language and that what is correct or wrong depends on what is formally accepted as grammatical. If you have ever heard of the slang term 'grammar Nazi', know

> that these are most likely people who are prescriptivists, and often ones who feel the need to impose their own prescriptivism upon others!
>
> **Linguistic descriptivism**, on the other hand, is non-judgemental. It is the stance that there is no correct or wrong way to use a language, but rather it is concerned with understanding how language is used in real life and describing that phenomenon. Linguists and sociolinguists in most instances take a descriptive approach to linguistics rather than a prescriptive one. We are not interested in telling people what they ought to be doing but rather understanding what is possible in human language. If there were only one way of doing things, then there would be no variation, and the world would be very boring to linguists.

In this chapter on multilingualism, status planning is a lot more relevant than corpus planning. In that regard, language policies are a set of ideas and legislation that are conceived and implemented to bring about specific sorts of language behaviours in society. Most countries have official language policies that either promote or discourage the use of particular languages. This may include policies that designate a particular language or a set of languages as national and/or official and policies that stipulate which language or languages are taught at schools and are used as a medium of instruction. The national language is one that is used for the purpose of rallying the nation's citizenry, mired in that one language-one nation approach, which belies the fact that, in reality, multiple diverse languages are typically spoken on the ground. The official languages, then, are those that are used for official purposes such as governance, trade, commerce, education, and in some countries even the mainstream media.

For example, the national and official language of Malaysia is Bahasa Melayu, also known as Malay, while the national and official language of the Philippines is Filipino, also known as Tagalog (Rappa & Wee 2006). Interestingly, English is also used for H domains and functions in Malaysia and the Philippines, such as business and commerce, yet the language has official status in the Philippines but not across Malaysia, where it is recognised as an official working language only in the states of Sabah and Sarawak. In this matter, it has to be recognised that English is often seen to be desirable, particularly if the country wants to take part in the wider international economy, but what then happens to the indigenous languages (Rappa & Wee 2006)? Chapter 5 deals with questions like this in more detail. For now, note that Malay is not the only indigenous language of Malaysia, and Filipino is not the only indigenous language of the Philippines. Malaysia itself contains 111 living languages, their language families ranging from Austronesian to Aslian (Eberhard, Simons & Fennig 2023). The Philippines itself is said to contain 175 languages, mostly Austronesian (Eberhard, Simons & Fennig 2023). Complicating matters further, other languages that are not traditionally considered indigenous are spoken in these places. Other languages that are spoken in Malaysia include Mandarin and other Sinitic languages, as well as Tamil and other languages originating in India and a variety of contact languages such as Baba Malay and Malacca Creole Portuguese. Other languages in the Philippines include local varieties of Chinese as well as a number of Chabacano creole varieties. Which languages are represented officially and which are not becomes quite telling of the policymakers' priorities.

The role of language policies within the education system is a whole other matter altogether. These language policies clearly emphasise what languages are desirable for attainment. In multilingual countries, a multilingual education also becomes possible. As a case in point, Singapore practices what is known by some linguists as "English-knowing bilingualism" (Pakir 1994) (see previous section on mother tongue ideology). The main medium of education is English, but students are required to study a second language that represents their 'mother tongue'. Chinese students are required to learn Mandarin, Malay students are required to learn Malay, and Indian students are required to learn Tamil at the mainstream schools, regardless of whether these students actually do speak these 'mother tongue' languages at home. Such a policy undoubtedly does several things at once. It favours English as an international **lingua franca** (a common language that people of different backgrounds use to talk to one another) and the language through which knowledge is mostly accessed while simultaneously acknowledging the role of the Chinese economy, the fact that Singapore is surrounded by Malay-Muslim countries, and that most Indians from Singapore have come from a Tamil background. However, it also clearly homogenises speakers of other languages and views linguistic diversity as an issue for nation-building (Rappa & Wee 2006). Educational language policies are also built to further particular agendas, and it becomes clear that these top-down approaches often make no allowance for other minority languages within mainstream education.

3.2.5 Immersion

One way that has been utilised to reclaim the use of minority languages in countries that are open to doing so is through language immersion programmes. The immersion programme is a bilingual one that uses both a native language and second language media of instruction for various subjects, such as mathematics or history. Teachers are often bilingual, and immersion programmes aim to promote **additive bilingualism** (wherein one language is acquired in addition to another, not at the expense of another) (Johnson & Swain 1997). Note that the exact duration spent in each language or the subjects undertaken in each language may differ, but in general, the success of such programmes depends on the availability of resources as well as the commitment of decision-makers, teachers, and students (Cummins 1998). While the language immersion programme became popularised in the context of Canada, where native English speakers attended elementary schools where French was used as a medium of instruction, language immersion has also been used to revitalise endangered languages. For example, Hawai'ian language immersion schools were created by Hawai'i's Department of Education in the mid-1980s and are still successfully being run, in a reversal of the language's circumstances (Reyhner 2010). Other efforts to revitalise endangered languages through immersion include programmes for Māori in New Zealand (Spolsky 1989) and Scottish Gaelic in Scotland (Nance 2015), among others (see Chapter 5 for more details regarding language endangerment). In addition to **language revitalisation**, immersion language programmes have been used to help students adapt to mainstream education, particularly when their native language may not be the language of mainstream education. At the same time, it has become a lot more popular among people who simply want their children to learn a second language (Watanabe 2011).

3.3 How does a multilingual speaker juggle more than one language?

Just as societies deal with the presence of more than one language differently, so do individuals in terms of how they acquire these languages, how they function in these languages, what they can do with these languages, and even their attitudes towards being multilingual or towards the multiple languages that they speak.

3.3.1 Simultaneous acquisition versus sequential acquisition

Individuals are said to vary widely in terms of how they acquire an additional language. The terms in this section are bilingual-centric, given that the relevant research on individuals has mostly focused on people acquiring two languages and that the term 'bilingual' has also been used to refer to people who speak more than two languages (Grosjean 2010). A common myth, perhaps, is that most bilinguals acquire two or more of their languages at childhood, which would qualify them as being simultaneous bilinguals, when in fact most speakers of two or more languages are sequential bilinguals who acquired one language before another or others (Grosjean 1984; Grosjean 2010). While the actual dividing line can be unclear between simultaneous bilinguals and sequential bilinguals (is there a difference between a child hearing an additional language on the day of birth versus one who hears the additional language two weeks later?), most researchers actually regard simultaneous bilinguals as those who hear more than one language regularly from the first few days of life (Grosjean & Byers-Heinlein 2018). Additionally, it is notable that most people become bilingual because they are required to, whether it be due to immigration, marriage, education (Grosjean 2010), or other factors.

> **What sort of bilingual or multilingual are you?**
>
> If you are bilingual (or even multilingual, if you prefer this term), think about whether you would consider yourself a simultaneous bilingual or a sequential bilingual, and if you are a sequential bilingual, what made you pick up the additional language(s)? Did you have a choice?

3.3.2 Balanced bilingualism, subtractive bilingualism, and additive bilingualism

Yet another myth is that bilinguals are perfectly balanced and have equal knowledge and proficiency in both or all of their languages. The truth is that most bilinguals know their languages to the extent that they require them, and most can be dominant in one language while not knowing how to read or write in the other (Grosjean 2010). Bilinguals who have equal command of both languages constitute an extremely small minority (Grosjean 2010). In fact, it should become clear if you were to compare the kinds of things that you can do in the languages that you speak if you are bilingual or multilingual. Even if we could speak a second or a third language, most of us might not be comfortable doing math or chemistry in our second or third languages or, perhaps for some of us, in our native language, and that is perfectly normal.

Another way of looking at proficiency in the individual languages that a bilingual speaker commands considers if the acquisition of a second language adversely affects the individual's competence in their first language. **Subtractive bilingualism** refers to the situation when competence in the first language is affected by acquiring a second language. It was found that undergoing a school system that took place entirely in a second language was indeed detrimental to people in minority groups, in that their first language would be at some point replaced by this second language (Lambert 1975). However, the notion of subtractive bilingualism is often taken out of context in order to justify why it is not possible to be truly bilingual. We know that this is not the case, given the correct circumstances. **Additive bilingualism** is the other possible outcome of **sequential bilingualism**, in which one language is acquired after another. Additive bilingualism connotes positive consequences in the learning of a second language, in a situation where the first language continues to be valued while the second language is acquired. While learning in a second language was detrimental to the first language of minority groups, it was noticed that privileged speakers with a first language that had a high status in the community benefited from being taught in a second language (Lambert 1975). This sort of research exemplifies how important it is to understand the sociolinguistic circumstances of speakers before one can fully account for the effects of something such as bilingual education (Landry & Allard 1993). The contrasting outcomes also underscore the fact that languages are seldom equal in status (see Chapter 6 on language and justice) and that situations of bilingualism can exemplify that sort of inequality. Given the unequal status of languages, and with additive bilingualism as a goal, it has been suggested that groups with a vital first language undergo immersion in a second language, while groups with a much less vital first language undergo schooling in that first language (Landry & Allard 1993).

3.3.3 Language attitudes towards multilingualism

At the individual level, instead of looking at language ideologies which are shared beliefs, we are looking at **language attitudes**, which may be shaped by larger language ideologies or beliefs about languages. Attitudes towards multilingualism are usually categorised as either being positive or negative.

Negative attitudes can be held within traditional monolingual societies, where bilinguals might be perceived as individuals with conflicting personalities who harbour unclear political allegiances, in which these attitudes are often associated with anti-immigration sentiments (Dewaele 2015). Parents themselves may also fear that their own language may be holding back their children in mainstream schools. Relatedly, some education systems provide a bilingual education in the minority speakers' home language, but with the long-term aim of transitioning them into a monolingual system. Such an attitude towards bilingualism contrasts with those who are economically better off. Particularly, **elite bilingualism** can be practised, where well-educated, upwardly mobile individuals are proficient in widely used world languages (Mejía 2002) and where parents and individuals see an education in a second language as being useful for providing one with immense socioeconomic opportunities—opening up markets and opportunities that would otherwise not be available to the monolingual speaker.

3.4 The brains, minds, and emotions of multilingual speakers

Another perspective on multilingual speakers themselves comes from a cognitive perspective. While this is a book primarily about sociolinguistics, it is useful to look at the claims surrounding multilingualism from the cognitive stance, as this helps us better understand societal and individual attitudes towards multilingualism. So, what goes on in the minds and brains of multilingual speakers? An older question that people were and are interested in is whether speaking a second or third or fourth language made one more intelligent. Part of what has shifted people's attitudes towards a more positive take on multilingualism comes from the growing body of research that shows that there are cognitive benefits to being multilingual.

3.4.1 Are multilinguals more intelligent?

Multilingualism wasn't always seen as a good thing. Specifically, bilingualism was viewed as something that would lead to confusion over language choices and even "retardation". As a case in point, a widely used textbook on child psychology in America had stated that "there can be no doubt that the child reared in a bilingual environment is handicapped in his language growth" (Hakuta 1986: 367 citing Thompson 1962). Early studies that support such a stance, however, have been criticised for their flawed methodology, for example, requiring the bilinguals to do the IQ tests in their weaker language, among other missteps.

Intelligence perhaps is too broad a term, and studies that concern the cognitive benefits of multilingualism approach the term from a variety of angles. Studies have shown that bilinguals have better executive control, which comprises processes such as inhibitory control (ignoring irrelevant information), working memory (retaining and manipulating information), and cognitive flexibility (switching between tasks) (Bialystok, Craik & Luk 2012). Bilinguals also showed slower cognitive aging when compared to monolinguals, particularly so when responding to a task which required participants to not be disrupted by incongruent items when these were presented (Bialystok et al. 2004).

The Simon task

The task that was used in the previous study on cognitive aging was the Simon task, which showcases the Simon effect. There are a few versions online for use. Find one and try it out.

Additionally, a range of studies have shown that bilinguals have greater **metalinguistic awareness**, which refers to the ability to solve problems on language based on one's knowledge of linguistic forms, structures, meanings, and cross-linguistic equivalents (for example, the awareness that English has tense but Mandarin does not, among myriad other issues) (Bialystok, Craik & Luk 2012: 240).

Overall, modern literature tells us that there are a lot of cognitive benefits to being bilingual or even multilingual and that being multilingual is far from going to hurt us cognitively.

3.4.2 Do multilinguals have split personalities?

There is no real support for the notion that multilinguals have different personalities, although some people who speak more than one language may feel that one language may make them feel more polite, while another makes them feel harsher (Grosjean & Pavlenko 2021). It is clear that most assertions such as these are anecdotal at best. Instead of viewing the multilingual as problematic individuals with split personalities, modern research suggests that what they do have is an "enhanced repertoire of possibility" (Edwards 2013: 20). Just as a speaker of one language may vary the use of that language according to their environment, interlocutors, topic, and so on, "bicultural bilinguals" may adapt attitudes, feelings, and behaviours (along with language) to the environment, culture, and interlocutors around them; there is no direct causal relationship between language and personality in the least bit (Grosjean & Pavlenko 2021: 205); and this is far from a good reason to appeal against multilingualism. Cognitively and emotionally, then, it appears that there are only benefits to be had where multilingualism is concerned.

3.5 Effects of multilingualism on language itself

Aside from discussing the effects and non-effects that multilingualism can have on the brains, minds, and emotions of the multilingual speaker, another venue for study is the effects of multilingualism on language itself. Multilingualism can manifest in multiple ways, including codeswitching and codemixing, translanguaging, the borrowing of loanwords, and even the borrowing of structures across languages.

3.5.1 Codeswitching and codemixing

Codeswitching refers to the use of more than one language within a single conversation (Myers-Scotton 1995). It must be said that codeswitching is not something people do because they are lazy (Grosjean 2010) but because they are able to! Codeswitching can be part of strategic communication.

In the following scenario, a customer is codeswitching from English to colloquial Malay while he speaks to a Malay-speaking cooked food vendor at a hawker centre in Singapore.

Customer: Can I have steamed fish, long beans, and an egg, and curry over the rice?
Vendor: OK.
Customer: *Banyak kuah boleh-kan, kak?*
"Can I have a lot of gravy, older sister?"

Now, the customer clearly codeswitched here to accommodate to the Malay speaker, in hopes of getting more gravy with his rice. But the social reasons for codeswitching can go beyond simply getting what one wants. Here is an excerpt from Myers-Scotton (1995: 134) that shows a bus conductor switching from Swahili to English. The English portion is italicised.

Conductor: Umelipa nauli ya basi?
"Have you paid the bus fare?"
Passenger: (No response)
Conductor: Unaenda wapi?
"Where are you going?"
Passenger: Nafika Jerusalem.
"I am going to Jerusalem [housing estate]."
Conductor: *You must always say clearly and loudly where you are going to alight, OK?*

Why do you think the bus conductor codeswitched from Swahili to English? Your guess is as good as mine. Do you think English allowed him more distance and superiority when instructing the passenger? Swahili clearly would not have had the same effect.

Then there are other patterns, such as these ones, where the italicised words are in Mandarin.

Mother (to a child): Are you *tuzi or a duck?*
"Are you a bunny or a duck?"
Teacher (to a colleague): I decided to *kankan zai dasuan.*
"I decided to look at how things go before deciding."

These sorts of insertion patterns may sometimes appear by other names, such as **insertion** or even **codemixing**. In the example of the mother, she has inserted the Mandarin word for "bunny" where the English word could appear, presumably as her daughter is more familiar with the Mandarin term. In the instance of the teacher talking to her colleague, she inserted a Mandarin phrase where an English one (such as "wait and see"), could appear. She wasn't able to explain to me why she had done so when, as an observer, I pointed this out to her. This example shows that codeswitching is not always entirely consciously done, although subconsciously, she must have been aware that her interlocutor understood both languages.

The important thing here is that phenomena such as the ones described here do not usually come about because of one's incompetence in one language but rather demonstrate some level of social awareness and a high level of linguistic competence in cognitively juggling the two or even more languages that one may speak!

3.5.2 Translanguaging

It should have become apparent reading this chapter that a multilingual speaker has multiple resources in their toolkit when simply doing anything at all with language and that these speakers are able to deploy whichever language is more suitable for the purpose at hand in order to make sense of the world and interact with it (Wei 2018). **Translanguaging** treats the multiple languages that a speaker can have as belonging to the same single system (Vogel & García 2017), instead of an approach that treats two or more languages as being distinct, separate systems. It acknowledges how fluidly and dynamically speakers can transit between languages as they require. Interestingly, the notion of translanguaging came about and is popular in the applied field of education, where it refers to a sort of pedagogical approach which allows the use of more than one language in the classroom, particularly so in a bilingual classroom where both languages can be utilised for all purposes and in all domains (García 2009). A simple example might be when I use Mandarin in my classroom to reinforce concepts in linguistic typology to my graduate students who are Chinese nationals because they seem to understand the terms more comprehensively when I use Mandarin. Rather than viewing them as being less competent in one language, translanguaging acknowledges that Mandarin might be more appropriate to foster a fuller understanding of what is being covered at that moment. Of course, there are different extents to which translanguaging can be carried out in the classroom or even outside of it. You might ask at this point: what, then, is the difference between codeswitching and translanguaging? The two seem similar but are essentially different in the number of systems that they recognise. While codeswitching recognises two different systems or more, given that it is defined as alternating between languages, translanguaging treats the multiple resources that a multilingual speaker can have as a single system. Note that while research shows the value of translanguaging in encouraging a fuller and deeper understanding of the academic subjects (Lewis, Jones & Baker 2012), the value of a bilingual classroom, or even a multilingual one, can still be debatable in societies that may value monolingualism above all else.

3.5.3 Loanwords

Beyond codeswitching and translanguaging, multilingualism can make its effect felt more permanently. If your first language is English, do you know that on a daily basis, or even an hourly basis, you are using words that originate from another language? The Norman invasion of England in 1066 (that lasted 116 years) was perhaps the most influential, with French becoming the language of administration and culture for a while. For example, do you know that words such as 'café', 'beef', 'mutton', 'pork', 'judge', 'evidence', 'sport', 'modern', 'liberal', and 'civilisation' (and this is very far from an exhaustive list) all come from French? Of course, outside of war and invasion, with any contact situation between speakers of multiple languages, words can be borrowed from any source language into any target language. The technical term for the phenomenon is really a misnomer, because no one expects a language to ever return anything that was borrowed, and borrowing really is far from temporary. Once a **loanword** makes its presence felt, it is pretty much there to stay, for reasons such as the fact that the loanword represents an item or concept that may not have previously existed in the culture or that the loanword is a fancier way of saying something—for example, saying 'pork' to refer to the meat of the animal specifically, instead of just 'pig', which refers to the animal itself. Other languages also abound with examples. In Japanese, *aisu* means 'ice', and *apaato* means 'apartment', these having been borrowed from English. And then there are words such as *chanpuruu*, which refers to an Okinawan stir fry dish and comes from the Malay word *campur* (the initial sound here being a CH, even though it looks orthographically different), which means 'mix'. Often loanwords are adapted to fit the phonological templates of the language that does the borrowing, phonological template here indicating the types of sounds and sequences of sounds that are permitted in the language, which explains why *aisu kurimu* still sounds Japanese! Loanwords exist in all sorts of languages. As a case in point, try out this short exercise.

Exercise: McDonald's by any other name: loanword or?

What is McDonald's (yes, the fast-food brand) called in different languages of the world? How many of these would you consider loanwords? Why or why not?

3.5.4 Structural borrowing

Beyond loanwords, structure can also be borrowed, although it is believed that such borrowing requires even more intense contact between speakers of different languages and thus that **structural borrowing** as such is rarer. But it is not impossible, as some had previously believed. Structural borrowing can take place in different aspects of a language. Parts of a sound system, as well, can be borrowed. For instance, the Burmese phonological system has become more like the Mon phonological system, which is not surprising since a significant number Burmese speakers actually have a Mon background. As an example, the nuclei (or most sonorous part of a syllable) [ai] (pronounced AY) is not typically Burmese but can be attributed to Mon loanwords, or Shan and Thai to a lesser extent, these being languages that Burmese speakers also encounter (Bradley 1980). Grammatical parts of speech can also be borrowed. Due to the invasion of Norse-speaking Norwegians and Danes in parts of England around the 9th century, a number of grammatical traits were borrowed, including the pronouns 'they', 'them', and 'their', which replaced Old English equivalents *hie/he:o*, *him/hira*, and *heom/heora*, respectively, as well as the strong forms for certain verbs, such as 'give' in *gaf and geeven* (which are of course equivalent to 'gave' and 'given' today) (Winford 2003: 80). These are just a couple of examples. We will see how structural borrowing can be even more pervasive when the intense contact of two or more languages leads to the emergence of what we know as contact languages (see Chapter 4).

References

Académie Française. 2024. *Questions de langue | Acaémie française*. www.academie-francaise.fr/questions-de-langue#12_strong-em-anglicismes-et-autres-emprunts-em-strong. (16 February, 2024).

Alisjahbana, Takdir. 1949. The Indonesian language-by-product of nationalism. *Pacific Affairs*. University of British Columbia 22(4). 388–392.

Anderbeck, Karl. 2015. Portraits of language vitality in the languages of Indonesia. In I Wayan Arka, Ni Luh Nyoman Seri Malini & Ida Ayu Made Puspani (eds.), *Language Documentation and Cultural Practices in the Austronesian World: Papers from 12-ICAL, Volume 4*, 19–47. Canberra: Asia-Pacific Linguistics.

BBC. 2022. French officials told to abandon gaming Anglicisms. *BBC News*, sec. Technology. www.bbc.com/news/technology-61647192. (16 February, 2024).

Bialystok, Ellen, Fergus I. M. Craik, Raymond Klein & Mythili Viswanathan. 2004. Bilingualism, aging and cognitive control: Evidence from the Simon task. *Psychology and Aging* 19(2). 290–303. https://doi.org/10.1037/0882-7974.19.2.290.

Bialystok, Ellen, Fergus I. M. Craik & Gigi Luk. 2012. Bilingualism: Consequences for mind and brain. *Trends in Cognitive Sciences* 16(4). 240–250. https://doi.org/10.1016/j.tics.2012.03.001.

Bloomfield, Leonard. 1933. *Language*. New York: Henry Holt and Co.

Bradley, David. 1980. Phonological convergence between languages in contact: Mon-Khmer structural borrowing in Burmese. *Proceedings of the 6th Meeting of the Berkeley Linguistic Society* 6. 259–257.

Cummins, J. 1998. Immersion education for the millennium: What have we learned from 30 years of research on second language immersion? In M. R. Childs & R. M. Bostwick (eds.), *Learning through Two Languages: Research and Practice* (Second Katoh Gakuen International Symposium on Immersion and Bilingual Education), 34–47. Japan: Katoh Gakuen.

Dewaele, Jean-Marc. 2015. Bilingualism and multilingualism. In *The International Encyclopedia of Language and Social Interaction*. https://doi.org/10.1002/9781118611463.wbielsi108.

Dickinson, Jennifer. 2010. Languages for the market, the nation, or the margins: Overlapping ideologies of language and identity in Zakarpattia. *De Gruyter Mouton* 2010(201). 53–78. https://doi.org/10.1515/ijsl.2010.004.

Eberhard, David M., Gary F. Simons & Charles D. Fennig. 2023. *Ethnologue: Languages of the World*. 26th edition. Dallas, TX: SIL International. www.ethnologue.com.

Edwards, John. 2013. Bilingualism and multilingualism. In Tej K. Bhatia & William C. Ritchie (eds.), *The Handbook of Bilingualism and Multilingualism*, 5–25. Wiley-Blackwell.

Eriksen, Thomas Hylland. 1992. Linguistic hegemony and minority resistance. *Journal of Peace Research*. SAGE Publications Ltd 29(3). 313–332. https://doi.org/10.1177/0022343392029003007.

Ferguson, Charles A. 1959. Diglossia. *Word* 15(2). 325–340. https://doi.org/10.1080/00437956.1959.11659702.

Fishman, Joshua A. 1965. Who speaks what language to whom and when? *La Linguistique* 1(2). 67–88.

Fishman, Joshua A. 1967. Bilingualism with and without diglossia; diglossia with and without bilingualism. *Journal of Social Issues* 23(2). 29–38. https://doi.org/10.1111/j.1540-4560.1967.tb00573.x.

Fishman, Joshua A. 1972. *The Sociology of Language*. Rowley, MA: Newbury House Publishing.

Fishman, Joshua A. 1987. Conference comments: Reflections on the current state of language planning. In Lorne Laforge (ed.), *Actes du colloque international sur l'aménagement linguistique, 24–29 mai 1986/Ottawa* (Travaux du Centre international de recherche sur le bilinguisme, A-21 [Pulications of the International Centre for Research on Bilingualism, A-21]), 407–428. Québec: Les Presses de l'Université Laval.

Fujita-Round, Sachiyo & John C. Maher. 2017. Language policy and education in Japan. In Teresa McCarty & Stephen May (eds.),

Language Policy and Political Issues in Education (Encyclopedia of Language and Education), 1–15. Cham: Springer International Publishing. https://doi.org/10.1007/978-3-319-02320-5_36-2.

Fuller, Janet M. 2013. *Spanish Speakers in the USA*. Multilingual Matters.

Fuller, Janet M. 2018. Ideologies of language, bilingualism, and monolingualism. In Annick De Houwer & Lourdes Ortega (eds.), *The Cambridge Handbook of Bilingualism* (Cambridge Handbooks in Language and Linguistics), 119–134. Cambridge: Cambridge University Press. https://doi.org/10.1017/9781316831922.007.

García, Ofelia. 2009. Education, multilingualism and translanguaging in the 21st century. In Tove Skutnabb-Kangas, Robert Phillipson, Ajit K. Mohanty & Minati Panda (eds.), *Social Justice through Multilingual Education*, 140–158. Multilingual Matters. https://doi.org/10.21832/9781847691910-011.

Grosjean, François. 1984. *Life with Two Languages: An Introduction to Bilingualism*. Cambridge, MA: Harvard University Press.

Grosjean, François. 1997. The bilingual individual. *Interpreting* 2(1–2). 163–187.

Grosjean, François. 2010. *Bilingual: Life and Reality* (Bilingual: Life and Reality). Cambridge, MA, US: Harvard University Press. https://doi.org/10.4159/9780674056459.

Grosjean, François & Krista Byers-Heinlein. 2018. Bilingual adults and children: A short introduction. In François Grosjean & Krista Byers-Heinlein (eds.), *The Listening Bilingual: Speech Perception, Comprehension, and Bilingualism*, 4–24. Hoboken, NJ: John Wiley & Sons.

Grosjean, François & Aneta Pavlenko. 2021. *Life as a Bilingual: Knowing and Using Two or More Languages*. Cambridge University Press.

Hakuta, Kenji. 1986. *Mirror of Language: The Debate on Bilingualism*. Basic Books.

Harper, Martin. 2013. *One Nation, One People, One Language: The Story of Indonesia & Bahasa Indonesia*. Eum.

Hebblethwaite, Benjamin. 2021. Haiti's Foreign language stranglehold. *ForeignPolicy*. https://foreignpolicy.com/2021/08/03/haiti-language-education-school-french-haitian-creole/. (13 September, 2023).

Horner, Kristine & Jean Jacques Weber. 2008. The language situation in Luxembourg. *Current Issues in Language Planning*. Routledge 9(1). 69–128. https://doi.org/10.2167/cilp130.0.

Johnson, Robert Keith & Merrill Swain. 1997. *Immersion Education: International Perspectives*. Cambridge: Cambridge University Press.

Jonker, Louis C., Angelika Berlejung & Izak Cornelius (eds.). 2021. *Multilingualism in Ancient Contexts: Perspectives from Ancient Near Eastern and Early Christian Contexts*. 1st edition. Stellenbosch: African Sun Media. www.jstor.org/stable/j.ctv1nzfzj0. (27 June, 2023).

Keane, Webb. 2003. Public speaking: On Indonesian as the language of the nation. *Public Culture* 15(3). 503–530.

Kircher, Ruth & Ethan Kutlu. 2023. Multilingual realities, monolingual ideologies: Social media representations of Spanish as a heritage language in the United States. *Applied Linguistics* 44(6). 1077–1099. https://doi.org/10.1093/applin/amac076.

Lambert, Wallace E. 1975. Culture and language as factors in learning and education. In A. Wolfgang (ed.), *Education of Immigrant Students*. Toronto: Ontario Institute for Studies in Education.

Landry, Rodriguez & Real Allard. 1993. *Beyond Socially Naive Bilingual Education: The Effects of Schooling and Ethnolinguistic Vitality on Additive and Subtractive Bilingualism*. https://eric.ed.gov/?id=ED360866. (17 October, 2023).

Lewis, Gwyn, Bryn Jones & Colin Baker. 2012. Translanguaging: Developing its conceptualisation and contextualisation. *Educational Research and Evaluation*. Routledge 18(7). 655–670. https://doi.org/10.1080/13803611.2012.718490.

Mejía, Anne-Marie de. 2002. Elite bilingualism as sociocultural phenomenon. In *Power, Prestige and Bilingualism: International Perspectives on Elite Bilingual Education*, 51–74. Bristol/Blue Ridge Summit: Multilingual Matters. https://doi.org/10.21832/9781853595929-006.

Myers-Scotton, Carol. 1995. *Social Motivations for Codeswitching: Evidence from Africa* (Oxford Studies in Language Contact). Oxford/New York: Oxford University Press.

Nance, Claire. 2015. 'New' Scottish Gaelic speakers in Glasgow: A phonetic study of language revitalisation. *Language in Society*. Cambridge University Press 44(4). 553–579. https://doi.org/10.1017/S0047404515000408.

Pakir, Anne. 1994. Educational linguistics: Looking to the East. In James Alatis (ed.), *Georgetown University Round Table on Languages and Linguistics*, 370–383. Washington, DC: Georgetown University Press.

Pattanayak, Debi Prasanna. 1990. *Multilingualism in India*. Clevedon/Philadelphia: Multilingual Matters.

Pujolar, Joan. 2007. Bilingualism and the nation-state in the post-national era. In Monica Heller (ed.), *Bilingualism: A Social Approach* (Palgrave

Advances in Linguistics), 71–95. London, UK: Palgrave Macmillan. https://doi.org/10.1057/9780230596047_4.

Rappa, Antonio L. & Lionel Wee. 2006. *Language Policy and Modernity in Southeast Asia: Malaysia, the Philippines, Singapore, and Thailand*. New York: Springer.

Reyhner, Jon. 2010. Indigenous language immersion schools for strong indigenous identities. *Heritage Language Journal*. Brill 7(2). 299–313. https://doi.org/10.46538/hlj.7.2.7.

Sim, Cheryl. 2016. *Bilingual policy*. National Library Board Singapore. www.nlb.gov.sg/main/article-detail?cmsuuid=82fbbca5-e8e2-40cc-b944-fbb2bd2367fe. (2 July, 2024).

Spolsky, Bernard. 1989. Maori bilingual education and language revitalisation. *Journal of Multilingual and Multicultural Development*. Routledge 10(2). 89–106. https://doi.org/10.1080/01434632.1989.9994366.

Thompson, George. 1962. *Child Psychology*. Houghton Mifflin.

Vogel, Sara & Ofelia García. 2017. Translanguaging. In *Oxford Research Encyclopedia of Education*. https://doi.org/10.1093/acrefore/9780190264093.013.181.

Watanabe, Teresa. 2011. Dual-language immersion programs growing in popularity. *Los Angeles Times*, sec. California. www.latimes.com/local/la-xpm-2011-may-08-la-me-bilingual-20110508-story.html. (29 September, 2023).

Wei, Li. 2018. Translanguaging as a practical theory of language. *Applied Linguistics* 39(1). 9–30. https://doi.org/10.1093/applin/amx039.

Winford, Donald. 2003. *An Introduction to Contact Linguistics*. Oxford: Blackwell Publishing.

Chapter 4

Contact languages

4.1 What is a contact language?

In the last chapter, it should have become apparent that multilingualism is really a norm rather than an anomaly. We also came across ways in which multilingualism can bring about different sorts of changes in language use, such as through the borrowing of loanwords or even structure. In this chapter and the next, more extreme types of language change are broached. At one end of the continuum of possible change is the emergence of contact languages. A contact language comes about when people come into an intense period of contact with others who do not speak the same language as themselves. They may have come together for purposes such as trade and intermarriage, or perhaps they might have been forced by circumstances to be in a situation where inter-language communication would have been both functional and necessary. What results in that sort of situation is known as a '**contact language**', though the type and nature of the contact language vary greatly and depend on factors such as the intensity of contact and the sociological environment in which the language develops. The outcome of these multilingual encounters can be a pidgin (more unstable than a creole), a mixed language (these are more stable than a pidgin), and other sorts of contact languages that are less easily categorised (see next section for these definitions).

4.2 Different types of contact languages and their origin stories

One crucial thing to take note of is that scholars who engage in **contact linguistics** have different and strong opinions about how different types of contact languages are defined and what counts as a pidgin, a creole, or a mixed language. While many of these points surrounding their definitions may be debatable to specialists in the field, they can be a good starting point for discussion. It is also important to consider how linguists approach the prototypical pidgin, creole, and mixed language, so that we are aware of more interesting, diverse scenarios. Relatedly, the narratives behind the emergence of these contact languages which are born out of their sociohistorical circumstances show that it is impossible to appreciate a language fully without understanding the society or societies in which it evolves.

4.2.1 Pidgins

A **pidgin** is a language that results when groups of speakers with no language in common are compelled by circumstances to develop a "a common means of communication" (Thomason & Kaufman 1988: 167). The resultant pidgin appears to be a blend of two or more languages. If you were to speak only one of these component languages, you might be able to make smart guesses but most likely will not be able to understand the pidgin properly. While the pidgin may be perceived by some to be a corrupt or even broken version of a language, there is nothing broken or incorrect about it at all—it has its own set of rules, even if it is highly variable, and is not improvised on the spot in any ad hoc manner. Crucially, it is often nobody's first language, meaning it is seldom learnt at home by young children. You may also ask, why is a pidgin called a 'pidgin'? The term was first recorded in English in Canton (modern-day Guangzhou), China, in 1807 and may have its origins in the term 'business', in the Cantonese phrase *bei chin* 'pay money', or from the use of both terms (Li 2011). Another less popular term that has been previously used to refer to pidgins but did not gain traction is a 'jargon'. You may have heard of Mobilian Jargon, which was used as a common means of communication by different Native American groups living along the Gulf Coast of Mexico. Technically a pidgin, Mobilian Jargon was used to facilitate trade between these groups of Native Americans and European traders.

A pidgin that is less well known compared to Tok Pisin (its famous counterpart in Papua New Guinea that is used as the country's lingua franca) is Hiri Motu. It is a simplified version of the Motu language, with influences from Tok Pisin, English, as well as other languages spoken in the country. It may have had a precursor in a trading language used by the Motu people with the people that they came into contact with, but there was a version of Hiri Motu that was much more extensively used by the police, to the extent that some were calling it Police Motu (Dutton 1985). The language has since lost its currency as the language of the police, with usage of Tok Pisin becoming far more common than Hiri Motu, even though it still is one of the national languages of Papua New Guinea.

Yet another interesting pidgin is Chinook Wawa, also known as Chinook or Jargon, which began as a trading language in the Pacific Northwest region of North America, spreading from the lower Columbia River to parts of Oregon and Washington, and then British Columbia and Alaska, northern California, Idaho and Montana. The language was based in large part on Chinook and Nuu-chah-nulth (Nootka), among other indigenous languages, but also had input from French and to some extent English. While some believe that the language developed as an intra-indigenous language of communication before the arrival of the Europeans, others believe that the language developed as a means of communication between the Indigenous people and European settlers; it is also plausible that there might be truth in both accounts (Harris 1994). Unlike Hiri Motu, Chinook Jargon became further expanded into a first language for some speakers in British Columbia but is now critically endangered (Selkirk 2018). Notably, a number of languages that are termed jargons are actually pidgins, such as Slavey Jargon, Eskimo Trade Jargon, and Mobilian Jargon, to name a few.

Crucially, pidgins, due to how they have evolved, are thought of as being less elaborate in form and quite variable but sufficient to meet the functional needs of their speakers.

4.2.2 Creoles

Often spoken about in the same breath as pidgin is the notion of a **creole**. A creole traditionally refers to a pidgin that has gained native speakers (Holm 1989), meaning it is taught as a first language to children. However, it is now clear that this may be not a good criterion because there are pidgins that have gained some native speakers, such as Chinook Jargon, just as there are pidgins that have never gained native speakers and creoles that have no evidence of ever having been a pidgin (Velupillai 2015). Another plausible way of thinking about creoles is that they have gained **vernacularisation** (Chaudenson 1974), wherein the language becomes the common everyday language of use amongst a people. Creoles are therefore also thought of as being more grammatically elaborate than pidgins (Winford 2003), since they are further developed, with wider use. Beyond language, note that the word "creole" has related meanings in referring to a certain type of culture, such as the Louisiana Creole culture, and/or people, such as the Louisiana Creole community. Unsurprisingly, your knowledge of the word "creole" may or may not be limited to creole cuisine, given that cuisines are essential part of cultures. Importantly, what this shows is that creole languages have often arisen within a community in tandem with an entire culture. The most prototypical origin stories behind creoles often revolve around slavery and maroonage and the plantation. For instance, Haitian Creole emerged due to contact between enslaved Africans and French settlers in the colony of Saint Domingue (present-day Haiti) during the 17th and 18th centuries. The language has a largely French vocabulary, and other languages that have contributed to its structure include West African languages, Bantu languages, Spanish, English, and to some extent Amerindian languages such as Arawak-Taíno and Tupi (Fattier 2013). Relatedly, but in a different context of freedmen, Sierra Leone Krio, which is a mix of English, West African languages, and other European languages, arose when descendants of liberated slaves settled in a British colony for freed slaves between the 18th and 19th centuries and mingled and even intermarried with other settlers and Europeans, leading to a **creole** ethnicity and language (Dixon-Fyle & Cole 2006).

A different sort of creole is one that is born out of maroonage and mutiny. Here, maroonage refers to deliberately attempting to escape from slavery or colonialisation in a quest for freedom. An example of a creole that emerged from pure mutiny, however, is Pitkern or Pitcairnese, which emerged when British mutineers (from HMS Bounty) stopped over in Tahiti and took Tahitian women over to settle on Pitcairn island in the 18th century (Mühlhäusler 2011). It was suggested that a pidgin must have been formed so that these people who spoke different languages could communicate, and the language then would have expanded into a **creole** when children began learning the language as their first language. The language is critically endangered today.

Yet another type of creole is the plantation creole, which would have emerged on plantations when labourers from different language backgrounds would have had to interact with each other and with the owners and foremen. A famous example of such a creole would be Hawai'i Creole (also known as Pidgin). A chief locus of contact was the sugar plantation—labourers were brought in from the Atlantic islands of Portugal and East Asia, particularly southern China, Japan, Korea and the Philippines. They spoke their own languages, while the plantation owners and foremen would mostly speak English. A pidgin would have had been formed for communication, but as children of different backgrounds started using the language in schools and at the playgrounds, a much more stabilised and expanded creole was formed (Velupillai 2013).

Sociohistorically, while creoles have many different sorts of origin stories, there are often a few commonalities between these origin stories. There would have been a traumatic sort of geographical displacement of the creators and unequal social relations between the people who have to some extent acquire a new language and the speakers of that particular language (c.f. Ansaldo, Lim & Mufwene 2007), with the learners being less privileged (imagine: the slave or the labourer would have been the one who would had to acquire the language of the slave owners or plantation managers, not the other way around).

The slave trade triangle

Can you look up a map of the slave trade triangle? Can you also find out what creoles are spoken within this triangle and if these creoles have their origins in slavery?

Creole and Cajun?

The public perception of creole is sometimes limited to Creole cuisine, which is often talked about in the same breath as Cajun food. Now that you know what the term 'creole' refers to, find out who the Cajuns are.

4.2.3 Mixed languages

While a pidgin or a creole can comprise more than two languages, as the examples in the earlier section would attest to, a **mixed language** commonly comprises just two languages. A mixed language is usually not very simplified, because at least one of the two speaker groups would have been highly bilingual in both languages and doesn't need to simplify things. A mixed language is also easily separable into its two language components, although the division between the language components can vary. For example, Michif, spoken by the descendants of Nakota and Ojibwe-speaking women and French-speaking fur traders in the Saskatchewan and Manitoba regions of Canada and the North Dakota and Montana regions of the United States combines Cree verb phrases with French noun phrases (Bakker 1997). In a different sort of combination, Ma'a (also known as Mbugu), spoken in Tanzania by a nomadic group that moved into a region surrounded by Bantu languages, combines Bantu grammar with Cushitic lexicon (Mous 2003). Several reasons are posited for the development of **mixed languages**. It is said that they emerge during times of "significant social change" and serve as "an expression of a new identity or the maintenance of an older identity" (Meakins & Stewart 2022: 310). In the instance of Michif, the language came about as a way of expressing the identity of the new mixed-heritage community formed between the Indigenous women and fur traders. Likewise, Ma'a is said to have been created as a marker of a non-Bantu ethnic identity (Mous 2013). On the other hand, languages such as Light Walpiri and Gurindji Kriol (both spoken in Australia) are said to have emerged as ways of maintaining older identities. Light Walpiri comprises Walpiri, Kriol, and Australian English, and even though the language is different from Warlpiri, it is used by the younger speakers to resist shifting completely to Kriol, which is the dominant English-based creole of the region (O'Shannessy 2005). Similarly, Gurindji Kriol contains Gurindji elements that can be perceived as expressions of a persisting Gurindji identity in the face of **language shift** towards Kriol. The language emerged during a land rights movement that saw the Gurindji people leading a struggle to regain control of their traditional lands (Meakins 2008).

Note that unlike creoles, mixed languages are not as much associated with a traumatic past of displacement or unequal social relations between groups of speakers.

4.3 The structure and formation of contact languages, especially creoles

With an understanding of why people had to come up with new languages, the next question to ask is how did they or do they do it? This is a fascinating question for many researchers because it gives us insight on how human minds work, which then tells us more about what human minds are capable of. Unsurprisingly, the field of contact languages sees a lot of heated debates to do with the structure and formation of these languages.

One of the largest disagreements is whether contact languages have the simplest grammatical structures in the world. While some state that all languages are equal in complexity, others such as McWhorter (2001) have claimed that the world's simplest grammars are creole grammars. Pidgins, which are supposedly less structured than creoles, have also been claimed to be even more simple than creoles (Escure 2009). In the same vein, another argument that is often challenged is that creole languages are structurally distinct from non-creole languages (Bakker et al. 2011). This is a position undertaken by renowned creolist Derek Bickerton (1984), who posited how creoles structurally came about, among others.

4.3.1 The language bioprogram hypothesis

Bickerton's stance was that while a rudimentary pidgin was spoken only by immigrants, a more complex creole emerged among the children of these immigrants who spoke different languages at home. These children would have had ample opportunities to interact at school and during play, thus shaping the emerging creole. He believed that the innate language acquisition abilities of the children must have played a part in the formation of this creole. In this regard, Bickerton was of the opinion that there must have been a complete break in language transmission, as he believed that the creole was not a form of language passed on from parent to child. His hypothesis became known as the **language bioprogram hypothesis**—'bioprogram' because he thought this had to do with children's cognitive abilities. Crucially, Bickerton states that because creoles such as the one in Hawai'i arose out of these innate abilities of children, the structure of creole in Hawai'i would be similar to other creoles in the world. By way of stating this, he listed twelve grammatical features that he thought were universal across all creoles. For example, he believed that creoles often had a subject-verb-object word order and that auxiliary verbs are used to indicate tense, modality, and aspect (for example, the use of *stei* in Hawai'i Creole to mean the progressive in a sentence such as *I stei go* 'I am going'). But of course, as highlighted right at the beginning of this section, these viewpoints are highly contested. For instance, while the bioprogram would suggest that creolisation happens rapidly because humans have a innate ability to develop these systems, others such as Roberts (1998) have pointed out linguistic evidence showing that Hawai'i Creole formed over more than a generation and not as rapidly as initially thought.

There is also a group of scholars who repudiate the simple creole view, stating that contact languages such as creoles are not less complex structurally (Aboh & Smith 2009) and that they are unexceptional (DeGraff 2003). Any attempts to describe them as "simpler" may unconsciously stem from a racist bias of European colonisers regarding what they perceived as the Africans' inability to learn European languages (Aboh & deGraff 2016). The stance taken by researchers who believe that creoles are completely unexceptional is usually that the creoles are simply learnt varieties of target languages that the community in question have been exposed to. Accordingly, there would be no break in transmission or no pattern of abnormal transmission in the creole's formation.

4.3.2 The founder principle

An influential notion in creole genesis that does not consider the creole exceptional is the **founder principle** (Mufwene 1996). It views the target variety that the new speakers were learning as being particularly important. Often, it would be the case that these new speakers were learning from speakers of non-standard varieties and that non-standard features were maintained in the new varieties that emerged. In the context of slavery, newer slaves would have been learning the language from earlier generations of slaves who had learnt some variety of the target language or from the European foremen who managed the slaves (these Europeans themselves were possibly not speaking a standard variety). Additionally, the language gene pool, as it were, would more easily preserve features that were shared among all the languages involved. The target language is often called the **lexifier language**, which denotes that it provides most of the words for the contact language.

You may also hear the term **superstrate language** being used to refer to this language, not surprisingly, with its connotation of the uneven power structure between the slave populations and the founder populations. The other language or languages involved in the mix would be those spoken natively by the populace aiming to acquire the target language. Usually referred to as the **substrate language**, this language can provide quite a bit of grammatical input to the emerging creole.

4.3.3 Substrate transfer or relexification

A different approach is, then, the **substratist** approach, which overall proposes that the substrate language has an important part to play in the structure of the emerging creole. Syntactic features and functions are transferred from the speakers' native languages to the creole. In one version of such a theory, Siegel (2003) posits that it is in the process of learning the target language and the use of that language that the features of one's native language are transmitted into the creole. A Hawai'i Creole example he cites is taken from Bickerton (1981: 67):

(1) *Get wan wahine shi get wan data.*

'There is a woman who has a daughter.'

In (1), *get* is used for both the existential ('is') as well as the possessive ('has'). Siegel (2000) shows that this cannot be attributed to English but to similar functions in Cantonese. The next two examples taken from Siegel (2000: 214) demonstrate the respective uses of *yáuh* in Cantonese as possessive and existential markers, showing that **substrate transfer** has taken place between one of the substrate languages, Cantonese, to the creole.

(2) *Kéuihdeih   yáuh   saām   go   jái.*
    They   have   three   CL[1] son
    'They have three sons.'

(3) *Nī   go   deihfōng   yáuh   mahntàih.*
    this CL   place   have   problem
    'There's something wrong with this place.'

Crucially, a large number of early labourers imported to Hawai'i were Chinese plantation workers who spoke Cantonese, and this is said to have had a major effect on the linguistic shape of Hawai'i Creole.

In another more extreme version of the substrate approach, syntactic and semantic features are retained from the substrate language, while the "phonetic strings" (in simpler terms, how the words are said) in the superstrate language are overridden by phonetic strings from the superstrate language to form the creole—the logic being that in the specific context of slavery, the slaves were not sufficiently exposed to the superstrate language for them to properly learn about the deeper syntactic and semantic features, but they could at least perceive the words used (Lefebvre 1998: 16). What is known as the **relexification hypothesis** is used to explain the structural similarities between Haitian Creole and its major substrate language, Fongbe (Lumsden 1999: 342):

Haitian:

(4) *M   voye   rad   la   pou   Mari*
    I   send   clothing   DET[2]   for   Mari
    "I send the clothing for the benefit of Mari."

Fongbe:

(5) *Báyí   sɛ́   àwù   i   dó   Ajwá*
    Bayi   send   clothing   DET   for   Ajwa
    "Bayi sent the clothing for the benefit of Ajwa."

While there are clearly different viewpoints pertaining to creole language formation, there are still some structural generalisations that can be made across a good number of contact languages. In most instances, pidgins and creoles usually have a lexicon that comes mostly from one language, while the grammar is inordinately affected by the substrate language. Beyond that, the shape of contact languages such as pidgins, creoles, and mixed languages can only be understood in conjunction with their sociocultural histories.

4.4 Curious cases

It becomes apparent from the previous section that even within individual categories of contact languages, the languages are very diverse.

More often than not, contact languages resist clear categorisation. Here we have a few other examples of these curious cases.

Yilan Creole, officially known as Yilan Han-hsi Atayal in Taiwan, is spoken in I-Lan county of northeast Taiwan. The language was formed when Taiwan was governed by Japan between 1895 and 1945, during which Japanese language education was introduced in the colony. At some point, there might also have been a Japanese-only policy in the villages, and those who were born in the earlier part of the 1900s would have acquired Japanese fluency (Tan 2023). The original indigenous language of these affected villages was Atayal, and a new contact language emerged that is a mixture of Japanese and Atayal. While the language has been called a "creole" by some scholars, more recent work shows that it is not easily characterised as a creole and that Yilan Creole resembles more closely a second language variety of Japanese.

Yet another language that cannot be easily classified is Sri Lanka Malay. Sri Lanka Malay came about with the deportation of a heterogenous group of speakers from Malaysia and the easternmost provinces of Indonesia through periods of Portuguese rule, Dutch rule, and British rule. These people, who were often deported together with their families, included political dissenters and soldiers brought in by the Dutch to combat native rulers, as well as convicts, slaves, and indentured labourers (Ansaldo & Lim 2014). The language was formed through contact between these speakers of different early Malay varieties and evolved in a multilingual ecology in which Sinhala and Sri Lankan Tamil were influential. Alongside the substrate and superstrate languages, the **adstrate languages** are also important to consider—adstrate languages being other languages that are not more prestigious or less powerful than the creole language but that also exert influence on the creole given that these are all languages that share the same ecology. Given the influence of its significant adstrates, Sinhala and Tamil, Sri Lanka Malay is said to have been radically restructured, with an increase in morphological (word formation) complexity and the development of a grammatical case system, these existing to a large degree in both adstrates (Ansaldo & Lim 2014). These characteristics of Sri Lankan Malay therefore make it a lot more complex than what most presume contact languages to be like.

Further southeast, Baba Malay is a contact language formed by early intermarriages between Chinese traders and indigenous women. As early as the 15th century, Hokkien-speaking Chinese traders were settling in the Malay Archipelago. As it was uncommon for women to travel out of China at that time, these traders ended up forming families with local women. The language that emerged out of these intermarriages—which became the home language of their descendants—is Baba Malay. Baba Malay derives its lexicon mostly from a variety of Malay, although there is also significant input from Hokkien and some input from other languages that were popularly spoken at the time of its formation, including Portuguese, English, and Dutch, among others. The grammar of the language is heavily influenced by Hokkien and, to some extent, Malay. Sociohistorically, Baba Malay has been viewed as anomalous, if it is even considered a creole. Afterall, the history of Baba Malay never involved the traumatic displacement of people or considerably unequal relations between two groups of people (Ansaldo, Lim & Mufwene 2007). The language also does not easily constitute a mixed language, where component languages are easily sieved into two categories. Both lexicon and grammar comprise more than one language, and neither the verb system nor the noun system is entirely derived from a single language. The language is also more complex than the typical creole, with grammatical categories such as relative clauses and different registers for coarseness and refinedness.

4.5 The functions and domains of contact languages

Contact languages are perceived as very functional languages, perhaps as most people have the impression that they arose as languages that served as a means of communication for people with no language in common.

4.5.1 The contact language as lingua franca

Indeed, some contact languages have become known for their utility. The most famous of these examples would be the ones that are utilised as a **lingua franca**, a language chosen to be a common language of communication for large groups of people who do not share a common language. While this definition is very close to that of a contact language, note that the lingua franca simply denotes that the language is widely spoken, whether it be for trade or other purposes—it does not immediately mean that the language is a contact language. For example, English is a lingua franca in today's modern economy, as is Mandarin in some parts of the world. And yet the original lingua franca was most likely a language used by medieval traders and by the Crusaders that survived through the 15th century as a **proto-pidgin** (McMahon 1994). A proto-pidgin can be thought of as an ancestor pidgin to other related pidgins, and any proto language is one that has to be reconstructed through linguistic methods, usually by comparing related languages that still exist. Known as 'Sabir', the proto-pidgin or its varieties were said to have been used as a common language of communication for trade and commerce in the Mediterranean basin. 'Lingua franca' is therefore used as a term for languages which serve wide purposes of communications such as these. While lingua francas do not refer particularly to contact languages today, some contact languages serve as significant lingua francas. For example, Tok Pisin is the most widely used language in Papua New Guinea, which has over 800 languages (Eberhard, Simons & Fennig 2023), and is also one of its official languages that is used in parliamentary debates (Smith & Siegel 2013). Yet another known contact language that is used widely enough to be considered a lingua franca is Nigerian Pidgin, which is used by over 75 million speakers across Nigeria for interethnic communication at venues such as marketplaces, workplaces, schools, and the military, so much so that it has become the main language of day-to-day communication for many (Faraclas 2013).

4.5.2 *The missing domains of a contact language*

More often than not, contact languages are absent from a number of domains, mostly official ones. In general, contact languages are perceived as less prestigious and as inferior versions of their lexifier languages. They are therefore often kept out of domains such as government and education. Even where creoles are used in the context of education, they are seldom used as a medium of education but as a subject itself. Kreol Morisien (spoken in Mauritius) is learnt in the classrooms as a heritage language, and Réunion Creole is learnt as a regional language (Angelo 2020). Where they appear as a medium of instruction, they might be limited to use among the lower levels before students go on to learn in another language of instruction at a higher level. For instance, in

Seychelles, while all learning until Key Stage 2 (or Primary 3) takes place in Seselwa, their French-based creole, English is added on as the language of instruction gradually past that level (Angelo 2020).

4.5.3 The contact language at home

A good number of contact languages are limited to their home domains or to communication within a particular ethnicity, as these have developed alongside identity, for example, in the case of intermarriages. This is the case for Baba Malay, spoken only by the Peranakan Chinese, and Malaccan Creole Portuguese, spoken only by the Portuguese Eurasians in the Malay Archipelago. These languages are usually used only between family members or between friends who share the same ethnic identities. Languages such as these are more quickly threatened given that they are not widely spoken, being traditionally limited to the home domain or to non-official domains. But we will get back to this later in Section 6.

4.5.4 Newer domains of the contact language

Meanwhile, while contact languages are usually brought up as being very functional, it is interesting to also consider other domains that some of these contact languages are finding themselves in (Ansaldo & Meyerhoff 2020). For example, creoles can be found in more artistic domains such as theatre. The use of Pidgin (also known as Hawai'i Creole) for theatre began as early as the mid-1930s through the scripting of Pidgin plays that were encouraged by a university professor for his English courses, as well as through the establishment of a theatre company, Kumu Kahua Theatre, which aimed to produce original works for and by the people of Hawai'i (Baker 2020). Further east in Macau, Patuá, a Portuguese-based creole which is critically endangered, is still used in the theatre, and Patuá theatre is listed as an intangible cultural heritage by official departments (Cultural Affairs Bureau 2024). Leaving Asia Pacific behind, we also see the use of contact languages in theatre in the Caribbean. In the late 1960s and 1970s, popular theatre that drew on Jamaican Creole was used to express the struggles of women in Jamaica. In Guadeloupe, theatre can feature both Kréyòl and French, with language choice patterns reflecting patterns and expectations of the society (i.e. with Kréyòl as the language of familiarity and frankness, while French is the language of formality and pretence) (Managan 2020).

Other art forms that contact languages find themselves in include music and literature. Creole music itself consists of multiple genres. Guadalupian Kréyòl is used in *gwoka* music for its nationalist movement, Tok Pisin is used in in Papua New Guinean *lokal* music, Jamaican Creole is associated with Rastafari and reggae, and Nigerian Pidgin is used in Afrobeat and Nigerian hip hop, among others (Managan 2020). Literature is also commonly produced in contact languages. Note that there is a difference between literature that was produced by the speakers for themselves and that which was produced by others for the consumption of others. A couple of instances of speakers producing their own literature include Peranakan Chinese authors producing translations of Chinese classics in Baba Malay in the late 1800s and early 1900s for the enjoyment of readers who could not read Chinese (Lee 2023), as well as a writer writing plays, poems, and newspaper columns exclusively in Hawai'i Creole as an act of defiance against notions such as creole speakers not being as smart as standard English speakers (Soong & Tonouchi 2020). Then there were the exaggerated portrayals made of creoles and their speakers by non-native speakers who had become familiar with these languages in the Caribbean, written for the entertainment of non-native speakers who found these features "exotic", in what could be deemed linguistic blackface (Corcoran & Mufwene 1998). In a similar vein, when we think about music, there also instances of White pop artists who benefit from the use of African American English, even though the language and its native speakers continue to bear the brunt of discrimination in most contexts (Davis 2017). This in itself is an interesting phenomenon.

Creole music

Find an example of creole music online. What about it do you think makes it 'creole' (perhaps its lyrics, theme, or the way it is played)?

Beyond the scope of the arts and literature, there are also emerging domains afforded by digitisation (Heyd 2020). While contact languages may or may not be accepted on official domains, they find themselves in public domains due to social media and mobile phone use. Available corpuses of contact languages include Singapore English WhatsApp messages (Gonzales et al. 2023) and an email corpus that captures codeswitching between Jamaican Creole and English (Hinrichs 2006). Often, the contact language is viewed as an additional language resource that the speaker or writer has that allows them to perform a separate identity. For example, the use of West African Pidgins in sub-Saharan Africa allows the writers to convey particular personas, such as being skilful (Deumert & Lexander 2013). Other than using the contact language to do these things, there are also venues on public domains that allow speakers and writers to discuss matters to do with their language, interact with others in their language (where it would otherwise be difficult to find interlocutors), or even perform vestiges of it, if it is a particularly endangered language. Venues include Facebook, WhatsApp, and Telegram groups and channels for Michif and Baba Malay, among others.

4.6 The threatened contact language

Where it comes to language endangerment, some scholars believe that contact languages are **doubly threatened** as compared to noncontact languages (Garrett 2012; Lee 2020a). There are multiple factors for why this might be so, including economic, political, demographic, and attitudinal factors.

Where economic and political factors are concerned, contact languages often lack economic power, as compared to the standard languages that exist alongside them. For instance, contact languages often emerge in the face of colonisation, and while decolonisation has taken place in many parts of the world, the economic and political structures that stay rooted are Westernised ones that benefit languages such as English, French, and Spanish but not their contact versions as much. For example, Standard English is promoted through the Speak Good English Movement in Singapore, as it is Standard English and not Singlish that is perceived to give Singapore its economic edge over global competitors for trade and commerce. Politically, then, governments can implement policies that may be detrimental to these languages. Even when the contact language is given some sort of official status, it almost never has the same unfettered use in all domains as a standard language (Lee 2017). For example, in Section 5, where we talked about the use of contact languages in education, we see that when a language is used in the educational domain, it is often studied in a limited scope as a subject but not used as a medium of education or used at lower levels as a bridge towards using some standard language as a medium of education at higher levels.

Where demographic factors are concerned, contact languages can lose their speakers when the social circumstances that led to their emergence change. For example, Chinese Pidgin English, which arose out of trade within the Pearl River Delta of Southern China, is no longer spoken, partly because English-medium education became a thing in the region, and partly because the Canton Trade within which it evolved had declined drastically (Ansaldo 2009). Other communities, such as the Baba Malay-speaking community, the Malacca Portuguese Creole-speaking community, and the Michif community, were formed due to intermarriage between speakers of different languages. Today, while intermarriage can and still does take place, for example, between Chinese men and Malay women in Singapore, these intermarriages no longer lead to the development of the Peranakan Chinese identity and culture. Later intermarriages that take place in completely different social circumstances outside of that critical time and space, even with the same ethnic profiles, can no longer be considered additions to the community (Lee 2020a). As the original community diminishes in size, community members can marry outside their own communities to partners who speak different home languages. The language that they then pass on to their children is seldom the contact language, which is spoken in limited domains and perceived to be a broken language.

This brings us to **language attitudes**. Attitudes towards contact languages are often polarised. Contact languages can be the source of some pride, mostly **covert prestige**. They are emblems of a group identity for speakers themselves, but speakers themselves can experience complicated emotions towards their own language because of overall poor perceptions of the language. As reflected in the previous section, contact languages are often perceived as inferior versions of their standard language counterparts. For instance, speakers of St. Lucian Creole French may believe that they are not speaking a real language but a broken version of French (Frank 2007). It is not surprising, then, that contact languages may be doubly threatened as compared to non-contact languages (Lee 2020a).

All of this is not to say that all contact languages are doubly threatened or endangered. In fact, there are contact languages that impinge upon the vitality of other languages. For example, in Papua New Guinea, Tok Pisin, a contact language, is often the target of language shift from other indigenous languages. Similarly, Nigerian Pidgin English is a large threat to virtually all indigenous languages in Nigeria (Essegbey forthcoming), as is Cameroonian Pidgin to languages within Lower Fungom in Cameroon (Good 2012). While a good number of contact languages lack any real economic and political power, it is still important to consider the individual circumstances of contact languages when talking about language vitality.

4.7 Sociolinguistics and the contact language

Before this chapter draws to an end, it is interesting to broach the role of sociolinguistics studies proper for pidgins, creoles, and other contact languages. These contact languages often develop and exist in complex sociolinguistic environments, in situations that are highly multilingual, and are often in **diglossic** relationships with their lexifiers (Meyerhoff 2021). It is therefore unsurprising that sociolinguistics itself can be a productive topic for those studying contact languages.

The creole continuum or diglossia

Contact languages such as creoles are observed to form natural continuums. The observation is that most people do not speak creoles in the exact same way. An individual's speech could sound more **acrolectal** (more similar to its superstrate or lexifier), more **basilectal** (more similar to its substrate language), or **mesolectal** (somewhere in between), and speakers are known to be able to span all or several of these levels. Such a system has been used to describe Jamaican Creole (Le Page 1960) and Guyanese Creole (Rickford 1987), among others. In some instances, we might also see a more distinct switch between two systems (recall H and L varieties from Chapter 3), such as a quantitative corpus study showing that educated Nigerian Pidgin English speakers can switch between Nigerian Pidgin English and forms that are found in Standard English (Deuber 2006).

There is a multitude of other ways in which sociolinguistics can be approached in contact languages. One study that takes the lens of codeswitching determines if codeswitching, pidginisation, or even creolisation is involved in the formation of an informal urban variety in Cape Town, South Africa, known as Tsositaal (Mesthrie & Hurst 2013). Other studies look at language use and attitudes, such as through using survey methods to figure out if Aruban Papipamento, spoken in Aruba, is under threat (Kester & Buijink 2023), or by using a more covert matched guise task to figure out how a particular feature is falling out of Baba Malay due to changing attitudes (Lee 2020b). A map-labelling task that requires participants to label and talk about the areas in which a language variety is spoken has also been used to study how people commonly perceive variation in Cavite Chabacano, which is spoken in the Philippines (Lesho 2018).

Newer approaches involve looking at the effects of digitisation, such as a study of sociolinguistic styling and authenticity when Jamaican Creole is used on an internet forum (Moll 2015) or finding ways to promote creole literacy, such as by using Scrabble for Haitian Creole (Hebblethwaite 2009). Just as sociolinguistics continues to evolve by using a multitude of approaches to look at a range of issues, so does sociolinguistics that focuses on contact languages.

Notes

1 CL here indicates a classifier.
2 DET here indicates the determiner.

References

Aboh, Enoch & Michel deGraff. 2016. A null theory of creole formation based on universal grammar. In Ian Roberts (ed.), *The Oxford Handbook of Universal Grammar*, 400–458. Oxford University Press. https://doi.org/10.1093/oxfordhb/9780199573776.013.18.

Aboh, Enoch O. & Norval Smith (eds.). 2009. *Complex Processes in New Languages*. Amsterdam: John Benjamins Publishing.

Angelo, Denise. 2020. Creoles, education and policy. In Umberto Ansaldo & Miriam Meyerhoff (eds.), *The Routledge Handbook of Pidgin and Creole Languages*, 286–301. London/New York: Routledge.

Ansaldo, Umberto. 2009. *Contact Languages: Ecology and Evolution in Asia*. Cambridge: Cambridge University Press.

Ansaldo, Umberto & Lisa Lim. 2014. The lifecycle of Sri Lanka Malay. *Language Documentation & Conservation* 7. 100–118.

Ansaldo, Umberto, Lisa Lim & Salikoko S. Mufwene. 2007. The sociolinguistic history of the Peranakans: What it tells us about "creolization." In Umberto Ansaldo, Stephen Matthews & Lisa Lim (eds.), *Deconstructing Creole* (Typological Studies in Language). vol. 73, 203–226. Amsterdam: John Benjamins.

Ansaldo, Umberto & Miriam Meyerhoff (eds.). 2020. *The Routledge Handbook of Pidgin and Creole Languages*. London: Routledge. https://doi.org/10.4324/9781003107224.

Baker, Tammy Hailiʻōpua. 2020. The rise of Pidgin theatre in Hawaiʻi. In Umberto Ansaldo & Miriam Meyerhoff (eds.), *The Routledge Handbook of Pidgin and Creole Languages*, 232–249. London/New York: Routledge.

Bakker, Peter. 1997. *A Language of Our Own: The Genesis of Michif, the Mixed Cree-French Language of the Canadian Métis*. Oxford: Oxford University Press.

Bakker, Peter, Aymeric Daval-Markussen, Mikael Parkvall & Ingo Plag. 2011. Creoles are typologically distinct from non-creoles. *Journal of Pidgin and Creole Languages*. John Benjamins Publishing Company 26(1). 5–42. https://doi.org/10.1075/jpcl.26.1.02bak.

Bickerton, Derek. 1981. *Roots of Language*. Ann Arbor: Karoma Publishers, Inc.

Bickerton, Derek. 1984. The language bioprogram hypothesis. *Behavioural and Brain Sciences* 7(2). 173–221.

Chaudenson, Robert. 1974. *Le lexique du parler créole de la Réunion*. Paris: Champion.

Corcoran, Chris & Salikoko S. Mufwene. 1998. Sam Matthew's Kittinian: What is it evidence of? In Philip Baker & Adrienne Bruyn (eds.), *St Kitts and the Atlantic Creoles: The Texts of Samuel Augustus Matthews in Perspective*, 75–102. London: University of Westminister Press.

Cultural Affairs Bureau, Macau. 2024. Patuá Theatre-intangible cultural heritage. *Património Cultural de Macau*. www.culturalheritage.mo/(X(1)S(0le2kkueiqpeabldggweueme))/en/detail/100031?Aspx AutoDetectCookieSupport=1. (20 May, 2024).

Davis, Sonoya. 2017. *All about Dat Bass or Linguistic Blackface: White Pop Artists and African American English*. Michigan: Eastern Michigan University Senior thesis.

DeGraff, Michael. 2003. Against creole exceptionalism (discussion note). *Language* 79(2). 391–410.

Deuber, Dagmar. 2006. Verbal structures: Aspects of variation in educated Nigerian Pidgin. In Ana Deumert & Stephanie Durrleman (eds.), *Structure and Variation in Language Contact* (Creole

Language Library), 243–261. Amsterdam: John Benjamins Publishing Company. https://doi.org/10.1075/cll.29.14deu.

Deumert, Ana & Kristin Vold Lexander. 2013. Texting Africa: Writing as performance. *Journal of Sociolinguistics* 17(4). 522–546. https://doi.org/10.1111/josl.12043.

Dixon-Fyle, Mac & Gibril Raschid Cole (eds.). 2006. *New Perspectives on the Sierra Leone Krio*. Peter Lang.

Dutton, Tom. 1985. *Police Motu: Iena Sivarai (Its Story)*. Papua New Guinea: University of Papua New Guinea Press.

Eberhard, David M., Gary F. Simons & Charles D. Fennig. 2023. *Ethnologue: Languages of the World*. 26th edition. Dallas, TX: SIL International. www.ethnologue.com.

Escure, Geneviève. 2009. Is verb serialization simple? Evidence from Chinese Pidgin English. In Nicholas Faraclas & Thomas Klein (eds.), *Simplicity and Complexity in Creoles and Pidgins* (Westminister Creolistics Series), vol. 10, 109–123. London: Battlebridge.

Essegbey, James. forthcoming. Language endangerment, documentation and revitalization. In Rainer Vossen & Gerrit J. Dimmendaal (eds.), *The Oxford Handbook of African Languages*. Oxford: Oxford University Press.

Faraclas, Nicholas. 2013. Nigerian Pidgin structure dataset. In Susanne Maria Michaelis, Philippe Maurer, Martin Haspelmath & Magnus Huber (eds.), *Atlas of Pidgin and Creole Language Structures Online*. Leipzig: Max Planck Institute for Evolutionary Anthropology. https://apics-online.info/contributions/17. (20 May, 2024).

Fattier, Dominique. 2013. Haitian Creole. In Susanne Maria Michaelis, Philippe Maurer, Martin Haspelmath & Magnus Huber (eds.), *The Survey of Pidgin and Creole Languages. Volume 2: Portuguese-Based, Spanish-Based and French-Based Languages*, 195–204. Oxford: Oxford University Press.

Frank, David B. 2007. We don't speak a real language: Creoles as misunderstood and endangered languages. *Talk presented at a Symposium on Endangered Languages*, College Park, MD, sponsored by the National Museum of Language.

Garrett, Paul B. 2012. Dying young: Pidgins, creoles and other contact languages as endangered languages. In Genese Marie Sodikoff (ed.), *The Anthropology of Extinction: Essays on Culture and Species Death*, 143–162. Bloomington/Indiana: Indiana University Press.

Gonzales, Wilkinson Daniel Wong, Mie Hiramoto, Jakob R. E. Leimgruber & Jun Jie Lim. 2023. The Corpus of Singapore English Messages (CoSEM). *World Englishes* 42(2). 371–388. https://doi.org/10.1111/weng.12534.

Good, Jeff. 2012. "Community" collaboration in Africa: Experiences from Northwest Cameroon. *Language Documentation and Description* 11. 28–58.

Harris, Barbara P. 1994. Chinook Jargon: Arguments for a pre-contact origin. *Pacific Coast Philology*. Penn State University Press 29(1). 28–36. https://doi.org/10.2307/1316345.

Hebblethwaite, Benjamin. 2009. Scrabble as a tool for Haitian Creole literacy: Sociolinguistic and orthographic foundations. *Journal of Pidgin and Creole Languages*. John Benjamins 24(2). 275–305. https://doi.org/10.1075/jpcl.24.2.03heb.

Heyd, Theresa. 2020. Pidgins and Creoles: New domains, new technologies. In Umberto Ansaldo & Miriam Meyerhoff (eds.), *The Routledge Handbook of Pidgin and Creole Languages*, 322–334. London/New York: Routledge.

Hinrichs, Lars. 2006. *Codeswitching on the Web* (pbns), vol. 147. Amsterdam: John Benjamins Publishing Company. https://benjamins.com/catalog/pbns.147. (21 May, 2024).

Holm, John A. 1989. *Pidgins and Creoles* (Cambridge Language Surveys), vol. 2. Cambridge/New York: Cambridge University Press.

Kester, Ellen-Petra & Samantha Buijink. 2023. Language use, language attitudes, and identity in Aruba: Is Aruban papiamento under threat? *Journal of Pidgin and Creole Languages*. John Benjamins 38(2). 389–430. https://doi.org/10.1075/jpcl.22010.kes.

Le Page, Robert. 1960. *Jamaican Creole*. London: Macmillan.

Lee, Nala H. 2017. The vitality or endangerment of some nonindigenous languages: A response to Mufwene. *Language* 93(4). e234–e242. https://doi.org/10.1353/lan.2017.0067.

Lee, Nala H. 2020a. The status of endangered contact languages of the world. *Annual Review of Linguistics* 6(1). 301–318. https://doi.org/10.1146/annurev-linguistics-011619-030427.

Lee, Nala H. 2020b. Utilizing the matched-guise as a method of examining perceptual change in an Endangered Creole. *Applied Linguistics* 42(2). 207–229. https://doi.org/10.1093/applin/amaa011.

Lee, Nala H. 2023. Variability or its loss in creole endangerment: The case of Baba Malay. *Asia-Pacific Language Variation* 9(1). 59–82.

Lefebvre, Claire. 1998. *Creole Genesis and the Acquisition of Grammar: The Case of Haitian Creole*. Cambridge: Cambridge University Press.

Lesho, Marivic. 2018. Folk perception of variation in Cavite Chabacano. *Journal of Pidgin and Creole Languages*. John Benjamins 33(1). 1–47. https://doi.org/10.1075/jpcl.00001.les.

Li, Michelle. 2011. *Chinese Pidgin English and the Origins of Pidgin Grammar*. Hong Kong: The University of Hong Kong PhD dissertation.

Lumsden, John S. 1999. Language acquisition and creolization. In Michael DeGraff (ed.), *Language Creation and Language Change: Creolization, Diachrony and Development*, 129–157. Cambridge: MIT Press.

Managan, Kathe. 2020. Creole arts and music. In Umberto Ansaldo & Miriam Meyerhoff (eds.), *The Routledge Handbook of Pidgin and Creole Languages*, 217–231. London/New York: Routledge.

McMahon, April. 1994. *Understanding Language Change*. Cambridge: Cambridge University Press.

McWhorter, John H. 2001. The world's simplest grammars are creole grammars. *Linguistic Typology* 5. 125–126.

Meakins, Felicity. 2008. Land, language and identity: The socio-political origins of Gurindji Kriol. In Miriam Meyerhoff & Naomi Nagy (eds.), *Social Lives in Languages—Sociolinguistics and Multilingual Speech Communities: Celebrating the Work of Gillian Sankoff*, 69–94. Amsterdam: John Benjamins. https://espace.library.uq.edu.au/view/UQ:219382. (18 January, 2019).

Meakins, Felicity & Jesse Stewart. 2022. Mixed languages. In Anna Maria Escobar & Salikoko Mufwene (eds.), *The Cambridge Handbook of Language Contact. Volume 2: Multilingualism in Population Structure* (Cambridge Handbooks in Language and Linguistics), 310–343. Cambridge: Cambridge University Press. https://doi.org/10.1017/9781009105965.016.

Mesthrie, Rajend & Ellen Hurst. 2013. Slang registers, code-switching and restructured urban varieties in South Africa: An analytic overview of tsotsitaals with special reference to the Cape Town variety. *Journal of Pidgin and Creole Languages*. John Benjamins 28(1). 103–130. https://doi.org/10.1075/jpcl.28.1.04mes.

Meyerhoff, Miriam. 2021. Variation in Pidgin and Creole languages. In Umberto Ansaldo & Miriam Meyerhoff (eds.), *The Routledge Handbook of Pidgin and Creole Languages*, 348–362. London/New York: Routledge.

Moll, Andrea. 2015. *Jamaican Creole Goes Web: Sociolinguistic Styling and Authenticity in a Digital "Yaad"*. (cll), vol. 49. Amsterdam: John Benjamins Publishing Company. https://benjamins.com/catalog/cll.49. (28 May, 2024).

Mous, Maarten. 2003. *The Making of a Mixed Language: The Case of Ma'a/Mbugu*. Amsterdam: John Benjamins.

Mous, Maarten. 2013. Mixed Ma'a/Mbugu. In Susanne Maria Michaelis, Philippe Maurer, Martin Haspelmath & Magnus Huber (eds.),

The Survey of Pidgin and Creole Languages. Volume 3: Contact Languages Based on Languages from Africa, Asia, Australia, and the Americas. Oxford: Oxford University Press. https://apics-online.info/surveys/62. (1 November, 2023).

Mufwene, Salikoko S. 1996. The founder principle in creole genesis. *Diachronica* 13(1). 83–134.

Mühlhäusler, Peter. 2011. Some notes on the ontology of Norf'k. *Language Sciences* (Linguistics Out of Bounds: Explorations in Integrational Linguistics in Honour of Roy Harris on His 80th Birthday) 33(4). 673–679. https://doi.org/10.1016/j.langsci.2011.04.022.

O'Shannessy, Carmel. 2005. Light Warlpiri: A new language. *Australian Journal of Linguistics* 25(1). 31–57. https://doi.org/10.1080/07268600500110472.

Rickford, John R. 1987. *Dimensions of a Creole Continuum.* Stanford: Stanford University Press.

Roberts, Sarah. 1998. The role of diffusion in the genesis of Hawaiian Creole. *Language* 74(1). 1–39.

Selkirk, Diane. 2018. North America's nearly forgotten language. *BBC.* www.bbc.com/travel/article/20181002-north-americas-nearly-forgotten-language. (30 October, 2023).

Siegel, Jeff. 2000. Substrate influence in Hawai'i Creole English. *Language in Society* 29(2). 197–236.

Siegel, Jeff. 2003. Substrate influence in creoles and the role of transfer in second language acquisition. *Studies in Second Language Acquisition* 25(2). 185–209. https://doi.org/10.1017/S0272263103000093.

Smith, Geoff P. & Jeff Siegel. 2013. Tok Pisin structure dataset. In Susanne Maria Michaelis, Philippe Maurer, Martin Haspelmath & Magnus Huber (eds.), *Atlas of Pidgin and Creole Language Structures Online.* Leipzig: Max Planck Institute for Evolutionary Anthropology. http://apics-online.info/contributions/22. (7 July, 2017).

Soong, Micheline M. & Lee A. Tonouchi. 2020. Creoles in literature: Talking story with Lee A. Tonouchi, 'Da Pidgin Guerrilla' on Pidgin in the local literatures of Hawai'i. In Umberto Ansaldo & Miriam Meyerhoff (eds.), *The Routledge Handbook of Pidgin and Creole Languages,* 250–268. London/New York: Routledge.

Tan, Gan-ling. 2023. A new view on 'Yilan Creole'. *Journal of Pidgin and Creole Languages.* John Benjamins 38(2). 320–388. https://doi.org/10.1075/jpcl.00115.tan.

Thomason, Sarah G. & Terrence Kaufman. 1988. *Language Contact, Creolization, and Genetic Linguistics.* Berkeley/Los Angeles: University of California Press.

Velupillai, Viveka. 2013. Hawai'i Creole. In Susanne Maria Michaelis, Philippe Maurer, Martin Haspelmath & Magnus Huber (eds.),

The Survey of Pidgin and Creole Languages. Volume 1: English-Based and Dutch-Based Languages. Oxford: Oxford University Press. https://apics-online.info/surveys/26. (31 October, 2023).

Velupillai, Viveka. 2015. *Pidgins, Creoles and Mixed Languages*. Amsterdam/Philadelphia: John Benjamins.

Winford, Donald. 2003. *An Introduction to Contact Linguistics*. Oxford: Blackwell Publishing.

Chapter 5

Language endangerment

5.1 What is language endangerment?

In the previous chapters, we dealt with multilingualism as well as the extreme outcomes of multilingualism in the form of contact languages. This chapter looks at the other end of the spectrum of possible change—when language endangerment and dormancy occur. **Language endangerment** occurs when a language's vitality is threatened. When a language loses its last speaker, we say that language has become **dormant**, mainly because there might be an undiscovered last speaker and because there might be some chance that a language can still be reawakened (more on this later). In much of the earlier literature, researchers spoke of the demise of a last speaker as **language death**. Now, we speak of it only if we are very certain that the language is indeed gone.

Language death is by no means a new phenomenon. Several languages that we know to have disappeared in the ancient past include Sumerian, Egyptian, and Etruscan, among others (Swadesh 1948). However, what has suddenly put language endangerment on the radar of linguists is the rate at which it is happening in this present day. In 1991, it was famously predicted that 50 to 90 percent of the world's existing, living languages would be in trouble by the end of the 21st century (Krauss 1992). More recent estimates show that one language falls out of use or becomes dormant every three months or so (Campbell et al. 2013). While numbers might not be as extreme as initial predictions have made it out to be, they are still alarming, given the huge problem that language loss entails for all stakeholders (virtually anyone who speaks or signs a language).

DOI: 10.4324/9781032621517-5

5.2 Why is language endangerment an immense problem?

Language endangerment is an immense issue for humanity, linguists, and members of the community.

5.2.1 The loss of language diversity

Language endangerment is a threat to **language diversity**. Each language represents a unique perspective on what the human mind is capable of. One language may feature lexical concepts that do not exist in other languages. Another may encode for a grammatical category that does not exist elsewhere. Losing those languages can mean that we will never be fully aware of what human cognition is capable of. For example, most languages have sentences in these forms: Subject-Object-Verb and Subject-Verb-Object, so most people might say 'Ali apple eats' or 'Ali eats apple' in their language (just as in Korean and English, respectively). Other patterns do exist, with the rarest being Object-Subject-Verb. This order exists only in a handful of languages in the world, such as Tobati and Xavante, which are spoken in Indonesia and Brazil, respectively. Then there are languages which encode for positional verbs. Instead of "the cup is on the table", Yélî Dnye, a Papuan language, uses "sit", "stand", and "hang" in the position of the 'is' copula (Ameka & Levinson 2007). If languages such as Tobati, Xavante, and Yélî Dnye are not spoken anymore, considering that these are endangered languages (Campbell & Belew 2018), then we would lose evidence that the human cognition is capable of such a word order or grammatical category.

5.2.2 The loss of an intellectual repository

In the same vein, losing a language also means losing part of the intellectual repository of human beings. Some languages have expressions denoting knowledge that is not encoded in the expressions of other languages. For example, Kallawaya, a language spoken in the Andes of Bolivia, encodes over 900 species of medicinal plants (Girault 1989). Today, the language is considered severely endangered (Hauk & Heaton 2018). If we were to lose languages such as these, then we would lose ecological and botanical information, as well as cultural knowledge. As more poetically put by Ross Perlin (2014) at the Endangered Language Alliance:

> Some languages may specialize in melancholy, or seaweed, or atomic structure, or religious ritual; some grammars may glory in conjugating verbs while others bristle with syntactic invention.

Languages are far more diverse than we think they are. If we believe that there are 7,000 languages in the world (estimates range between 5,000 and 80,000), then there really are "7,000 natural experiments in evolving communicative systems" (Evans & Levinson 2009: 432), and losing even one language would mean losing one important piece of the puzzle.

5.2.3 The loss of human history, familial history, culture, and identity

Similarly, languages are a repository of human history. If we lose a language, we lose the ability to reconstruct earlier stages of human history. For instance, certain forms of Neolithic signs such as the Indus script found in regions of South Asia, which date back to 4,000 years ago, remain undeciphered. Beyond a shared history, losing our own languages means losing the ability to comprehend our personal histories. If you do not speak the same language as your grandparent, which is completely plausible, how will you learn about your familial past, aside from what the parental generation might share, and that is if they share at all?

Culturally, languages can be viewed as a marker of cultural and/or ethnic identity. Hawai'i Creole is perceived as a marker of solidarity and local culture (Drager 2012), just as the Hmong-Mien languages reflect the ethnicity of their speakers (Ratliff 2007). If languages such as these are lost, then part of what constitutes ethnic and/or cultural identity will also be lost.

Think about: language, culture, and ethnicity

Can you find other examples of languages that are closely related to a culture or ethnicity? Do you think it would be possible

> for a person to be an X-man if they do not speak X-ish (in the words of Joshua Fishman)? In other words, is it possible to claim belonging to a particular culture or ethnicity if one does not speak the language associated with that culture or ethnicity?

5.2.4 Language and well-being

Relatedly, language loss has been shown to affect the psychological well-being of affected speakers (Hallett, Chandler & Lalonde 2007) as well as bringing about worse physical health outcomes in Indigenous populations (Flood & Rohloff 2018). In a similar vein, languages can be valuable for promoting community cohesion and vitality and fostering pride in one's culture, as well as in giving a community its sense of self-confidence (Crystal 2000: 31).

5.2.5 Language and biocultural diversity

As with any topic that deals with the social aspects of language, not everyone believes that languages are worth saving. To many, a language is not like the Javan rhinoceros or the mountain gorilla, even if the rate of endangerment for languages is comparable to the rate of endangerment for biological species. We have a 50 to 90 percent estimate for languages, while 41 percent of amphibians are threatened, followed by 37 percent for sharks and rays, and 26 percent for mammals; at the top of the list are cycads at 70 percent (IUCN 2024). Interestingly, there may be a correlation between the decline of linguistic diversity and cultural diversity and the loss of biodiversity, plausibly because 70 percent of the world's languages are found in geographical hotspots of biodiversity (think the Amazonian rainforests, for example) (Gorenflo et al. 2012). Another study suggests that there is a link between forest destruction and the loss of languages (Loh & Harmon 2014). Yet, for detractors, there might be other sorts of reasons to care. Some might believe that language change is normal, that new languages may be created or even uncovered. For what it is worth, languages are also not anyway near being created or uncovered at the same rate as the loss of languages (Lee 2020a). Others may believe that having many languages in general is wasteful for the world's economy, presumably because firms and individuals have to spend money on translating (Crystal 2000), and this would mean processes and interactions are less efficient than they could be in the minds of the people who think that way. But likewise, there might be others who believe that there are benefits to having many languages even in business, for example, through multilinguals having a broader perspective of things in general or greater social acceptance by more groups of people (Crystal 2000).

Of course, as this section should show, there are so many more compelling reasons for why we should care about losing languages than simply valuing languages for financial gain. It is worth noting that this volume was written during the years of UNESCO's proclaimed "Indigenous Languages Decade" (2022–2032). The proclamation recognises that most of the world's fast-disappearing languages are Indigenous ones, which jeopardises the cultures and knowledge systems of which they are a part. As UNESCO puts it, these languages "add to the rich tapestry of global cultural diversity", without which "the world would be a poorer place" (UNESCO 2022).

5.3 Why and how does language endangerment happen?

It has been recognised for a long time now that the reasons for language loss are non-linguistic rather than linguistic (Swadesh 1948)—meaning that sociological explanations are often key to understanding why language endangerment has taken place.

When a community of speakers begins to use another language in place of the original language that they used to speak, we say that **language shift** has taken place (Fishman 1964). There can be many reasons language shift takes place.

Language shift can take place because of economic and political factors, coupled with language attitudes and ideology that favour this shift (Belew & Simpson 2018). Speakers are often compelled to abandon their own language and shift to a different one for economic opportunities. For example, speakers of smaller languages may switch to English or Mandarin, perceiving these much larger and more popular languages as economic utility in a globalised economy, whether it be in a modernised job or in dealing with a much larger market that they deem to have more financial prospects. It should come as no surprise that English is an official language of many countries, even if it is not a language native to the place, such as in Nauru (where Nauruan is spoken natively) or Kiribati (where Gilbertese is spoken by most).

5.3.1 The role of language policies on language shift

Language shift is therefore also linked to political considerations, and policies can outright favour some languages over others or mean a lack of support for other languages. It should not come as a surprise that languages without institutional support, including those that have no place in the education system, are likely to be more threatened than those that are supported by mainstream policies, including educational policies. For example, in Inner Mongolia, Mandarin is now used even in ethnic schools as a medium of education. In other parts of China, even larger dialects can be affected by policies that favour Mandarin. Wu Chinese, for example, which is spoken by 80 million people, actually has the smallest group of active users aged between 6 and 20 as compared to other dialect groups surveyed (Ni 2022). **Language policies** can also be much more severe, outright banning certain languages from being used, such as the banning of Kurdish in the Ottoman Empire and the banning of the Ainu language after Ezo Island's (modern-day Hokkaido) annexation by Japan.

5.3.2 The role of language attitudes on language shift

Language shift, of course, does not happen solely because of policies. The attitudes of individual speakers are equally important. Attitudes can be affected by language policies which reflect some sort of official ideology, but in reality things are much more complicated than that. Pride, prestige, and even shame can be associated with individual languages. A sense of pride in one's language, social prestige, or even the notion that a language is suitable for use for a particular function can aid its survival, just as shame, low prestige, or the idea that one's language is "broken" and therefore unsuitable for use in various domains can lead to a language's demise (Lee 2020a). For example, we can recall the speaker of St. Lucian Creole French highlighted in Chapter 4, who stated, "We don't speak a language; we just speak broken French" (Frank 2007). Even though St. Lucian Creole French is used in interpersonal communication and in domains such as in speeches and sermons (Frank 1993), the language is still endangered. Likewise, Louisiana Creole French, having faced the brunt of racism and discrimination, is now critically endangered (Shahyd 2017). In extreme cases, Native American children were forced to attend American Indian boarding schools during the European Colonisation of North America which ran from the mid-17th to early 20th century. In addition to other atrocities, these children had their tribal names replaced with English names and were forbidden to use their own languages, and some had their mouths washed out with lye soap when they did so (Lomawaima, Child & Archuleta 2000). Understandably, speakers' personal experiences with their languages have an impact on their own perceptions of their language, and if a sense of inadequacy, shame, or trauma is attached to that language, it is more likely than not that the language will be restricted to lower unofficial domains (see Chapter 3) or outright lose speakers who have been discouraged from speaking it.

Abandoning a language is simply not something that people do out of choice. It is unlikely that speakers would be willing to give up their language and shift to another in the first place if their own language afforded them the same sort of opportunities as the languages that they have shifted to, if they were not discouraged or banned from speaking their language, or if there were no stigma or shame attached to it. However, while language shift accounts for a lot of language loss, it does not account for all of it.

5.3.3 Linguistic genocide

In very extreme cases, a language can be lost when native speakers are suddenly lost through wars or genocide, especially when language is used as a means of ethnic identification. Ubykh, a Caucasian language once spoken by the Ubykh people, lost a large number of its speakers through the events of the Circassian genocide that was caused by the Russian Empire, and those who were lucky enough to escape through deportation to the Ottoman Empire eventually shifted to other languages. In Brazil, the Akuntsú people who live in Rodônia state, Western Brazil, were mostly wiped out in the 1980s by cattle ranchers who wanted to use their land for their own purposes. When survivors were contacted in 1995, there were only seven Akuntsú people left (Aragon 2014), and today there are only three (Tavares 2023). Their language, belonging to the Tupari subfamily of Tupían, will unlikely outlive the natural lifespan of these speakers.

5.4 How do linguists talk about language vitality?

So, while we have come across terms such as 'endangered', 'critically endangered', and 'threatened', among others, how is it that linguists talk about these terms? In other words, how do linguists assess **language vitality**?

Any language that has a speaker population of less than 100,000 speakers is at risk; so says Michael Krauss, who is known for his prediction that 50 to 90 percent of the world's languages are at risk of disappearing by the end of this century (1992). While Krauss' predictions paint a highly catastrophic picture, which was ultimately necessary for very quickly raising awareness of language endangerment among linguists who are in a position to do something about it, language endangerment is more than a numbers game. Javanese, which is spoken by over 80 million speakers, is at risk by virtue of the fact that **intergenerational transmission** may not be taking place as much as it should be (Ravindranath & Cohn 2014), meaning that the language is not being passed on to the younger generation in particular. To understand why the language is not being passed on and find out how endangered a language is, we would have to look at sociological factors.

5.4.1 The Graded Intergenerational Disruption Scale and the Expanded Graded Intergenerational Disruption Scale

It might come as no surprise, with the factors for language shift and language endangerment being completely social in nature, that a sociolinguist would be the first to try to systematically approach language shift and language maintenance as a field of enquiry (Fishman 1964). Joshua Fishman introduced the seminal Graded Intergenerational Disruption Scale (GIDS), which is based on the notion that a language's vitality will be disrupted if intergenerational transmission is disrupted (1991). According to Fishman, intergenerational transmission is the most crucial factor for a language's vitality. He identified different domains of language use (such as education, mass media, government, education, the home, etc.) and devised a scale of eight levels, which ranges from a level 1 language that is used in education, work, mass media, and the government at the national level to a level 8 language whose only remaining speakers are members of the grandparent generation. The in-between levels represent the in-between stages, such as a level 3 language being one that is used for local and regional work by both insiders and outsiders and a level 6 language being one that is used orally by all generations and that is still being learned by children as their first language. An updated version of the GIDS is known as the Expanded Graded Intergenerational Disruption Scale (EGIDS) (Lewis & Simons 2010), as seen in Table 5.1, which comes with the following categories:

Table 5.1 Levels, labels, and descriptions on the EGIDS (adapted from Lewis & Simons 2010)

Level	Label	Description
0	International	The language is used internationally for a broad range of functions.
1	National	The language is used in education, work, mass media, government at the nationwide level.
2	Regional	The language is used for local and regional mass media and governmental services.
3	Trade	The language is used for local and regional work by both insiders and outsiders.
4	Educational	Literacy in the language is being transmitted through a system of public education.
5	Written	The language is used orally by all generations and is effectively used in written form in parts of the community.
6a	Vigorous	The language is used orally by all generations and is being learned by children as their first language.
6b	Threatened	The language is used orally by all generations, but only some of the child-bearing generation are transmitting it to their children.
7	Shifting	The child-bearing generation knows the language well enough to use it among themselves, but none are transmitting it to their children.

(*Continued*)

Table 5.1 (Continued)

Level	Label	Description
8a	Moribund	The only remaining active speakers of the language are members of the grandparent generation.
8b	Nearly Extinct	The only remaining speakers of the language are members of the grandparent generation or older who have little opportunity to use the language.
9	Dormant	The language serves as a reminder of heritage identity for an ethnic community. No one has more than symbolic proficiency.
10	Extinct	No one retains a sense of ethnic identity associated with the language, even for symbolic purposes.

Exercise: Assessing your own language on EGIDS

What would you say the level of your native language is on the EGIDS? If the language is between levels 0 and 6a, what do you think is helping it stay that way? If your language is level 6b and above, what factors do you think are contributing to its more threatened status on the EGIDS?

5.4.2 UNESCO's vitality factors

A different take on assessing language vitality is provided by UNESCO (see Table 5.2), which instead looks at nine different factors when assessing language vitality (UNESCO Ad Hoc Expert Group on Endangered Languages 2003).

What this approach shows is the importance of more nuanced and broader types of sociological information when trying to fully understand a language's vitality.

Table 5.2 UNESCO's nine factors for assessing language vitality (adapted from UNESCO Ad Hoc Expert Group on Endangered Languages 2003)

Factor number	Factor
1	Intergenerational language transmission
2	Absolute number of speakers
3	Proportion of speakers within the total population
4	Shifts in domains of language use
5	Response to new domains and media
6	Availability of materials for language education and literacy
7	Governmental and institutional language attitudes and policies, including official status and use
8	Community members' attitudes towards their own language
9	Type and quality of documentation

Exercise: How does your language respond to new domains and media?

Factor 5 of UNESCO's list of nine factors for assessing language vitality looks at how a language responds to new domains and media. What sort of new domains and media can you think of? Does your language feature in these new domains and media that you have brought up, and to what extent? Does the extent to which your language appears in these newer domains and media reflect its level of vitality? In other words, if your language appears only to a limited extent or does not feature at all in these domains, does it also mean that your language is equally threatened? If not, is the opposite true: If your language appears to the fullest extent in these domains, does it mean that your language is completely safe and viable overall?

5.4.3 The Language Endangerment Index

Besides GIDS, EGIDS, and the UNESCO approach, one of the newer ways of calculating language vitality is using the Language Endangerment Index (LEI), which aims to provide a level of endangerment regardless of how little information there might be about a language (Lee & Van Way 2016). This might be important if we need a birds-eye view of how endangered languages are globally, given that there is a lot we do not know beyond a language's name or the number of people purportedly speaking it. For example, very little is known about the Sentinelese language spoken on North Sentinel Island, which is located among the Andaman Islands. Very little is known about the people on that island, much less the language they speak, predominantly because they have been extremely hostile to those who have tried to land on their island, such as shooting at them with their bows and arrows, which led to the deaths of those who got close enough. However, a census which surveyed them from a distance showed that there might have been about 39 individuals on the island (India 2001). Therefore, while our notions of a language's vitality should be informed by as much sociological information as possible, it is sometimes not possible to do so, and other methods that utilise less information may be useful to consider. The LEI allows for this, seeking out only four types of information: (1) intergenerational transmission, (2) absolute number of speakers, (3) speaker number trends, and (4) domains of use. The overall evaluation of the language's vitality is crucially accompanied with a certainty scale. If all factors are utilised, we can say that we are 100 percent certain that the language is at the level of endangerment we say it is at. If fewer factors are used, then we can say that we are less certain, and so on and so forth. Overall, like the other frameworks, intergenerational transmission is the most important indicator of language endangerment. Without younger speakers learning the language, the language in question loses a viable future. Regarding speaker numbers, languages with smaller numbers of speakers are deemed more at risk than languages with larger numbers of speakers, for the most part. Regarding speaker number trends, whether speaker numbers are increasing or decreasing is also important. Finally, pertaining to domains of use, languages that are used in more domains are more viable than those that are restricted in usage. All of these are not new concepts but information that is usually more easily sought. Of course, other types of information, such as a speakers' attitudes, are also important, but this is usually less easily quantified across languages (see, however, Section 4.7, which covers sociolinguistics studies that can reveal attitudes towards languages undergoing shift).

5.4.4 Terms of language endangerment

Notably, the terms that are utilised to describe endangered languages are often debated. Some call the use of terminology such as language 'death' and 'extinction' defeatist and damaging (Perlin 2024). Others feel the same way about terms such as 'endangerment' and 'vulnerable'. In response, new categories are created. 'Awakening' is a category used to acknowledge languages that are dormant but where there exists some form of targeted language revitalisation overseen by a coherent group of people, with the goal of creating new speakers. Similarly, 'dormant' has been used for languages that are thought to have lost their last speakers recently or for any language where any doubt remains to the possible existence of speakers. Yet there is only a limited extent to which such terms can be utilised. The reality is that there must be some common way of talking about the real threats to language viability and that the terms used to talk about language endangerment must emphasise the magnitude of the language endangerment issue for them to be useful in raising awareness among community members, linguists, members of the public, policy-makers, and other stakeholders.

5.5 How can we help?—Language documentation

As a response to the high rates of language endangerment, linguists have been engaging in language documentation work. Modern-day language documentation work requires linguists to work together with the speakers of their languages for an extended period of time (months to years) so that they can come together to record their language accurately and to the fullest extent possible. In the past, those who conducted fieldwork were focused on describing the grammar of the language they were working on and would keep observations and records of the language in field notebooks. Sometimes there would be recordings made of these languages on audio cassette tapes. These notebooks and audio cassette tapes were kept for the purpose of the linguists so that insights could be derived for the study of the language, but not as much for the community whose language they captured. Additionally, these notebooks and tapes (if available at all) were often kept away in the attics, studies, and drawers, and with the passing of time and people, these records of the language were often forgotten. Even if they are found, they will likely be damaged or disintegrating; written or represented in some obscure, esoteric notation or theory; or completely inaccessible due to the formats they were recorded in— which of you readers reading this might have an audio cassette player at home, a CD player, or even a video cassette tape player (on the off chance that language use was more fully captured on video cassette tape recordings)? These formats have fast become obsolete in many households, and even if you were resourceful enough to get your hands on one of these devices, there is nothing to ensure that mould, mildew, and general degradation have not already gotten to that precious record of the language. And, of course, when that audio tape player finally works the way you want it to, it may not be clear what language the recording was in; which variety of the language it was in, if there are multiple varieties; where the recording might have taken place; who the speaker was; how old the speaker was at the time of recording; where the speaker was born; what other languages the speaker speaks; and so on (all of which, as sociolinguistics tells us, can make a difference to the form of the language recorded).

Do your audio and video recordings last forever?

Make a list of the audio and video recording formats that you know. How many years does each format last? You can most likely find this information on the Internet.

Modern language documentation tries to resolve the issues mentioned here, which is necessary considering that records made especially of endangered languages can often be helpful to the community who may want to use these recordings for other purposes (such as creating stories or pedagogical material), and these recordings can be the very last ones made of very critically endangered languages that are fast losing speakers. Modern **language documentation** focuses on the creation of records of a language that are multipurpose in nature, that are easily accessible to multiple users, and that are long lasting (preferably into perpetuity). What results from months to years in the field at this endeavour is usually a collection of high-quality audio recordings, annotated transcriptions that may be time-aligned to the audio recordings (meaning you know what was said at any point in the recording), and video recordings if available, as well as field notes in some instances and other material that the collector deems relevant to representing the language as fully as possible. Importantly, metadata (data about data) is kept regarding each item (with relevant demographic and social information of the speakers involved and even information about the topic being discussed at hand). File formats of recordings and even transcripts should be of high fidelity and easily accessible using various software, not just one program. Additionally, recordings and transcripts are made of a wide range of genres (including narratives and conversations, etc.), and the data that is collected is ideally represented in a way that can be understood by people without or with very little training in linguistics. This collection would usually be deposited in a digital archive—good examples of these are the Pacific and Regional Archive for Digital Sources in Endangered Cultures (paradisec.org.au) as well as the Endangered Languages Archive (elarachive.org), which seek to hold these collections as long as possible.

The data collected through modern language documentation efforts can be used for multiple purposes. These could be used to write reference grammars and dictionaries. They could be used for the analysis of syntax and morphology or for a sociolinguistics study. They could also be used to write teaching material such as textbooks and readers. They could be the basis of stories for children or the basis of plays for a general audience. The list is and should be extensive.

5.6 How can we help?—Language revitalisation

Beyond language documentation, **language revitalisation** is an important subfield in linguistics that allows linguists and community members to respond to language endangerment. In language revitalisation, the goal really is to reverse language shift by encouraging intergenerational transmission to take place. Language revitalisation can be led by linguists, community members, language activists, or other stakeholders. It can comprise various sorts of activities, including language use in formal and informal education, language classes, language nests, master-apprentice programmes (Wiltshire, Bird & Hardwick 2022), and language restoration workshops, among others.

5.6.1 Language classes

Language classes can take place at any level. These language classes can be led by individual members of the community or by community groups. For example, in Singapore, language classes on Chinese dialects are run by ethnic clan associations. Where pedagogical material is not available, as is the case for many endangered languages, revitalisation activities also incorporate the creation of such material, such as the development of a Baba Malay textbook and reader for these purposes (Chan 2018; Chan 2019). Language classes may also be adopted into parts of formal education. For example, Gamilaraay, Kaurna, and Wiradjuri, which are indigenous languages that are being revitalised in Australia, are taught as subjects at local universities. Outside of language classes, but still within the scope of the education system, language immersion schools (see Chapter 3) are a means towards language revitalisation. Language immersion schools have played a vital role in the revitalisation of the Hawai'ian language, which was once on the decline (Kapono 1995).

5.6.2 Language nests

Another concept that is very closely associated with the notion of providing an immersive language environment is that of the language nest. **Language nests** began as a concept for the revitalisation of Māori in New Zealand, where older speakers act as mentors for young children in early childhood programmes (Mita 2007). Such an activity directly tries to create a new generation of speakers and bolsters intergenerational transmission. The *Māori Te Kōhanga Reo* (*te*: definite article; *kōhanga*: nest; *reo*: language) in New Zealand is so successful that it has become a model for language nests elsewhere in the world, including Hawai'i and Finland.

5.6.3 Master-apprentice programmes

Yet another type of revitalisation activity, which also seeks to 'immerse' the learner in the language, is the **master-apprentice** language learning programme. The master-apprentice programme was first introduced in North America and involves a 'master' speaker and an 'apprentice' learner who work together in formal or informal setups (Hinton, Vera & Steele 2002). 'Apprentices' are highly motivated individuals, and 'masters' are ideally someone with whom 'apprentices' already have an existing personal relationship, such as a close family member or friend of the family. A set of guidelines are usually provided, and an appropriate time commitment is required for the programme to work, just as with all other language revitalisation activities. Unlike the immersion schools and language nests, such a programme is designed to work for languages with fewer people involved. It has also been adopted in places such as Australia and Finland (Pine & Turin 2017).

5.6.4 Breath of Life workshops

A notable programme in language revitalisation is the language restoration workshop, known as Breath of Life. These Breath of Life workshops involve both Indigenous people and linguists, by pairing a linguist mentor with each community group, so that Indigenous people learn how to utilise archival linguistic fieldnotes and recordings that may be available in their languages. To do so, they learn about basic linguistics, language teaching and learning, and revitalisation. Such programmes are vital for when the community groups involved have very few or no fluent speakers of their languages left (Baldwin, Hinton & Pérez-Báez 2018) and can be very useful when a record of the language still exists. The Breath of Life workshops have been successful at reintroducing or reawakening languages that may once have been dormant, such as the Nomlaki language (Maclay 2014).

5.6.5 Language revival through cultural revival

Beyond the programmes listed previously, another interesting programme is one that seeks to revitalise the language as part of a larger cultural revival movement. Youth in a local Black Tai school in Thailand are tasked to learn about their culture by working with experts in their community. By way of learning about their material culture, such as traditional embroidery or traditional hairdos, which would plausibly be much more interesting to the youth than just simply learning the language, they also encounter and learn their language. Not only do the youth become more knowledgeable about their ethnic culture and language, they also benefit by becoming more empowered as members of a marginalised community (Suraratdecha 2021).

As is clear, there are multiple ways of revitalising a language, all of which focus on creating new speakers, and most of which focus on intergenerational transmission. What is also clear is that there are multiple stakeholders involved in revitalising a language, and revitalisation programmes require sufficient motivation and, importantly, long-term commitment for the language to ultimately stand a chance against language shift.

5.7 Language variation and language endangerment

One of the more recent productive venues of research in language endangerment has centred on **language variation**. Years ago, the main sentiments regarding variation in endangered languages were that endangered languages had less variation than non-endangered, fully viable languages, and where there was variation, the variation tended to not be meaningful. There were also others who believed that linguists should be doing nothing but documenting these endangered languages, since doing anything else in a race against time would be a waste of time. Naturally, a lot is known about language variation in major languages, and important concepts in sociolinguistic variation have mostly been established from observing these major languages, but much less is known about language variation in minority and threatened languages (Hildebrandt, Jany & Silva 2017). With more work now being done on non-dominant languages, particularly in the field of language documentation, some of these earlier assumptions about variation in endangered languages have been debunked. Now we know that meaningful variation exists in endangered languages, which was not a stance researchers shared in the past (see Sections 7.2 and 7.3).

5.7.1 Why else should we study the sociolinguistics of endangered languages?

In addition to upping the representation of non-dominant languages in the discourse of sociolinguistics, there are other reasons why those who document languages should also consider sociolinguistic variation work. Both fields require a long-term ethnographic approach (see

Chapter 2). In sociolinguistic variation work, **ethnography** is required to figure out what locally meaningful social categories there can be that may not necessarily correspond to the social categories that we know in our own communities (Eckert 2012; Hay & Drager 2007). In language documentation, linguists are similarly encouraged to put aside their blinkers so that they can observe how languages may be used very differently from those they are familiar with (Hill 2006). Sociolinguistic studies that are well designed are also useful for understanding attitudes people have towards the languages that they speak in the context of language endangerment and are far more telling than self-reports (see Chapter 2). It isn't surprising, then, that more sociolinguistic variation work has been carried out on endangered languages in recent times. It can be interesting, for instance, to see how speakers of these languages maintain their identities through the linguistic variants even in the face of encroachment from more dominant languages (see the following sections for more).

5.7.2 Production in endangered languages

There are two ways we can classify sociolinguistic variation work on endangered languages: As mentioned, there is work that shows that these languages have meaningful variation, just like any other viable language out there. In a **production** study on a variety of Quechua spoken in Peru, researchers studied the alternation of the uvular phoneme in the past tense morpheme, /-rqa/ (the uvular is a sound that is articular with the back of the tongue and the flap of soft tissue that hangs down at the back of the mouth). Participants underwent a **sociolinguistic interview** as well as orally retold a story that they listened to aurally. What the research team found was that while the uvular form was most commonly used, speakers understood and used the non-uvular form, too, and that there might be a slight effect of the rural-urban divide, in which urbanites deleted the uvular more than rural speakers—the notion of being authentic being more apparent and important in the idealised form of the rural speakers (Povilonis & Guy 2022). Such a study contributes significantly to what we know about what motivates variation when attention is paid to speech when there is no formal standard form in the language. This is different from how people who speak a majority language with standard forms become more standard when they are paying attention to how they are speaking.

There is also work that demonstrates how variation may be occurring in the specific context of language endangerment or encroachment. A production study on Orchid Island in Taiwan tracks two patterns of AY and AW production in Yami, an Austronesian language. Older variants for words such as 'house/home' and 'sun, day' would be pronounced *vahay* [vaʁaɪ] and *araw* [aɹaʊ], respectively, whereas newer variants exist in *vahey* [vaʁəɪ] 'house, home' and *arew* [aɹəʊ]. The newer variants are raised, meaning that they are produced higher in the mouth than the older variants. The study elicits data from a range of participants across various ages and from different villages. The island is undergoing rapid economic transformation, shifting from fishing/farm to tourism. It is the younger islanders who would encounter outsiders more, and it is they who are leading the change, while older speakers are using the more conservative forms in general, thus contrasting an 'Other' identity with a traditional Yami identity (Lai & Gooden 2018), reminiscent of what was uncovered on Martha's Vineyard (see Chapter 2). In another study on Francoprovençal in France and Switzerland, a language that is secondary to French at both locales, palatalisation in production data is studied (palatalisation means that the front part of the tongue aside from the tip is drawn nearer the hard palate of the mouth than usual). In the past, palatalisation was only noted for /l/ when it occurred in certain onset clusters such as /kl, gl, pl, bl, fl/. Now, in performative-type speech, speakers were using palatalisation even in places where palatalisation would not have traditionally occurred. This is occurring as part of an emergent sociolinguistic norm among newer, less fluent speakers of the language, because palatalisation to them represents the idealised Francoprovençal. Essentially, such work shows that meaningful variation can also occur in language obsolescence (Kasstan 2019).

5.7.3 Perception in endangered languages

Other than production work, **perception** work has also been carried out on endangered languages. In Baba Malay, there are two forms of words encoding either coarseness or refinedness. Words ending with [-al], [-ar], and [-as] such as [tampal] 'mend', [bakar] 'burn', and [nanas] 'pineapple' are traditionally considered coarse, while their [ɛ] counterparts, [tampɛ], [bakɛ], and [nanɛ], pronounced TAMPAI[R], BAKAI[R], NANAI[R], traditionally convey refinedness. Language documentation work shows that younger and less proficient speakers are producing less refined forms than older speakers. A **matched guise task** (see Chapter 2) involves listeners hearing refined and coarse pairs of words produced by two speakers of the language and making evaluative judgements based solely on what is heard. Younger, less proficient speakers of the language perceived the refined form as being more emblematic of Baba Malay and its speakers. The coarse forms, on the other hand, which also exist in the mainstream Malay variety, were perceived not to be produced by speakers of Baba Malay. In an act of maintaining their identities, these younger speakers in particular, who were experiencing the brunt of language loss, appeared to be perceptually treating Baba Malay as being distinct and separate from Malay itself and creating new meanings for their coarse and refined language variants (Lee 2020b).

5.7.4 The importance of sociolinguistics work on endangered languages

People working in the field of language endangerment do not only contribute to understanding language variation and sociolinguistics in ways that cannot be gleaned from simply looking at viable, dominant languages. Documenting variation where it occurs can also address linguistic insecurity, particularly insecurities that may arise from being punished for speaking one's language, from younger speakers being less fluent than older speakers, and for community members whose identities may come into question when they don't speak the language. Documenting the different ways in which a language can vary and the different ways speakers use a language can be validating for community members who may feel insecure about the variety they speak or the variety that they feel they do not speak well (Abtahian & Quinn 2017). Sociolinguistic variation work in endangered languages can thus be fulfilling, particularly to the linguist who wants to make a difference in the community they serve.

References

Abtahian, Maya Ravindranath & Conor McDonough Quinn. 2017. Language shift and linguistic insecurity. *Language Documentation & Conservation* 13. 137–151.

Ameka, Felix K. & Stephen C. Levinson. 2007. Introduction: The typology and semantics of locative predicates: Posturals, positionals, and other beasts. *Linguistics* 45(5). https://doi.org/10.1515/LING.2007.025.

Aragon, Carolina Coelho. 2014. *A Descriptive Grammar of Akuntsú*. Manoa: University of Hawai'i Ph.D. dissertation.

Baldwin, Daryl, Leanne Hinton & Gabriela Pérez-Báez. 2018. The breath of life workshops and institutes. In *The Routledge Handbook of Language Revitalization*. Routledge.

Belew, Anna & Sean Simpson. 2018. Language extinction then and now. In Lyle Campbell & Belew, Anna (eds.), *Cataloguing the World's Endangered Languages*. London/New York: Routledge.

Campbell, Lyle & Anna Belew (eds.). 2018. *Cataloguing the World's Endangered Languages*. London/New York: Routledge.

Campbell, Lyle, Nala Huiying Lee, Eve Okura, Sean Simpson & Kaori Ueki. 2013. New knowledge: Findings from the catalogue of endangered languages. *Talk presented at the 3rd International Conference on Language Documentation and Conservation*, University of Hawai'i at Mānoa. http://scholarspace.manoa.hawaii.edu/handle/10125/26145. (25 December, 2021).

Chan, Kenneth. 2018. *Mari Chakap Baba: A Comprehensive Guide to the Baba Nyonya Language*. Singapore: Gunong Sayang Association.

Chan, Kenneth. 2019. *Chrita Chrita Baba*. Singapore: Wolf et al.

Crystal, David. 2000. *Language Death*. Cambridge: Cambridge University Press.

Drager, Katie. 2012. Pidgin and Hawai'i English: An overview. *International Journal of Language, Translation and Intercultural Communication* 1(1). 61–73.

Eckert, Penelope. 2012. Three waves of variation study: The emergence of meaning in the study of sociolinguistic variation. *Annual Review of Anthropology* 41. 87–100.

Evans, Nicholas & Stephen Levinson. 2009. The myth of language universals: Language diversity and its importance for cognitive science. *Behavioural and Brain Sciences* 32. 429–492.

Fishman, Joshua A. 1964. Language maintenance and language shift as a field of inquiry: A definition of the field and suggestions for its further development. *Linguistics*. De Gruyter Mouton 2(9). 32–70. https://doi.org/10.1515/ling.1964.2.9.32.

Fishman, Joshua A. 1991. *Reversing Language Shift*. Clevendon: Multilingual Matters.

Flood, David & Peter Rohloff. 2018. Indigenous languages and global health. *The Lancet Global Health*. Elsevier 6(2). e134–e135. https://doi.org/10.1016/S2214-109X(17)30493-X.

Frank, David B. 1993. Political, religious, and economic factors affecting language choice in St. Lucia. *International Journal of the Sociology of Language* 1993(102). 39–56. https://doi.org/10.1515/ijsl.1993.102.39.

Frank, David B. 2007. We don't speak a real language: Creoles as misunderstood and endangered languages. *Talk presented at a Symposium on Endangered Languages*, College Park, MD, sponsored by the National Museum of Language.

Girault, Louis. 1989. *Kallawaya: El idioma secreto de los incas [Kallawaya: The Secret Language of the Incas]*. La Paz, Bolivia: UNESCO-OPS-OMS.

Gorenflo, Larry J., Suzanne Romaine, Russell A. Mittermeier & Kristen Walker-Painemilla. 2012. Co-occurence of linguistic and biological diversity in biodiversity hotspots and high biodiversity wilderness areas. *Proceedings of the National Academy of Sciences of the United States of America* 109(21). 8032–8037.

Hallett, Darcy, Michael J. Chandler & Christopher E. Lalonde. 2007. Aboriginal language knowledge and youth suicide. *Cognitive Development* 22(3). 392–399. https://doi.org/10.1016/j.cogdev.2007.02.001.

Hauk, Bryn & Raina Heaton. 2018. Triage: Setting priorities for endangered language research. In Lyle Campbell & Anna Belew (eds.), *Cataloguing the World's Endangered Languages*, 259–304. London/New York: Routledge.

Hay, Jennifer & Katie Drager. 2007. Sociophonetics. *Annual Review of Anthropology* 36. 89–103.

Hildebrandt, Kristine A., Carmen Jany & Wilson Silva. 2017. Introduction: Documenting variation in endangered languages. *Language Documentation & Conservation* 13. 1–5.

Hill, Jane. 2006. The ethnography of language and language documentation. In Jost Gippert, Nikolaus P. Himmelmann & Ulrike Mosel (eds.), *Essentials of Language Documentation*, 113–128. Berlin: Mouton de Gruyter.

Hinton, Leanne, Matt Vera & Nancy Steele. 2002. *How to Keep Your Language Alive: A Commonsense Approach to One-on-One Language Learning*. Illustrated edition. Berkeley: Heyday.

India, Office of the Registrar General & Census Commissioner. 2001. *Census of India*. New Delhi: Government of India, Ministry of Home Affairs.

IUCN. 2024. *The IUCN Red List of Threatened Species*, Version 2023-1. www.iucnredlist.org. (18 June, 2024).

Kapono, Eric. 1995. Hawaiian language revitalization and immersion education. *International Journal of the Sociology of Language*. De Gruyter Mouton 1995(112). 121–135. https://doi.org/10.1515/ijsl.1995.112.121.

Kasstan, Jonathan R. 2019. Emergent sociolinguistic variation in severe language endangerment. *Language in Society* 48(5). 685–720.

Krauss, Michael. 1992. The world's languages in crisis. *Language* 68(1). 4–10.

Lai, Li-Fang & Shelome Gooden. 2018. The spread of raised (ay) and (aw) in Yami: From regional distinctiveness to ethnic identity marker. *Journal of Linguistic Geography* 6(2). 125–144. https://doi.org/10.1017/jlg.2018.8.

Lee, Nala H. 2020a. The status of endangered contact languages of the world. *Annual Review of Linguistics* 6(1). 301–318. https://doi.org/10.1146/annurev-linguistics-011619-030427.

Lee, Nala H. 2020b. Utilizing the matched-guise as a method of examining perceptual change in an endangered creole. *Applied Linguistics* 42(2). 207–229. https://doi.org/10.1093/applin/amaa011.

Lee, Nala H. & John Van Way. 2016. Assessing levels of endangerment in the Catalogue of Endangered Languages (ELCat) using the Language Endangerment Index (LEI). *Language in Society* 45(2). 271–292.

Lewis, M. Paul & Gary F. Simons. 2010. Assessing endangerment: Expanding fishman's GIDS. *Revue Roumaine de Linguistique* 55(2). 103–120.

Loh, Jonathan & David Harmon. 2014. *Biocultural Diversity: Threatened Species, Endangered Languages*. The Netherlands: WWF Netherlands.

Lomawaima, K. Tsianina, Brenda J. Child & Margaret L. Archuleta (eds.). 2000. *Away from Home: American Indian Boarding School Experiences, 1879–2000*. Heard Museum.

Maclay, Kathleen. 2014. Giving the "Breath of Life" to endangered languages. *Berkeley News*. https://news.berkeley.edu/2014/08/05/giving-the-breath-of-life-to-endangered-languages/. (20 June, 2024).

Mita, Deslie McClutchie. 2007. Maori language revitalization: A vision for the future. *Canadian Journal of Native Education* 30(1). https://doi.org/10.14288/cjne.v30i1.196401.

Ni, Vincent. 2022. Chinese dialects in decline as government enforces Mandarin. *The Observer*, sec. World news. www.theguardian.com/world/2022/jan/16/chinese-dialects-in-decline-as-government-enforces-mandarin. (11 June, 2024).

Perlin, Ross. 2024. Disappearing tongues: The endangered language crisis. *The Guardian*, sec. Science. www.theguardian.com/science/2024/feb/22/disappearing-tongues-the-endangered-language-crisis. (19 June, 2024).

Perlin, Ross. 2014. Radical linguistics in an age of extinction. *Dissent Magazine*. www.dissentmagazine.org/article/radical-linguistics-in-an-age-of-extinction/. (25 June, 2024).

Pine, Aidan & Mark Turin. 2017. Language revitalization. In *Oxford Research Encyclopedia of Linguistics*. https://doi.org/10.1093/acrefore/9780199384655.013.8.

Povilonis, Natalie & Gregory Guy. 2022. Authenticity in language ideology: Social variation in Chanka Quechua. *Asia-Pacific Language*

Variation. John Benjamins 8(2). 240–273. https://doi.org/10.1075/aplv.22004.pov.

Ratliff, Martha. 2007. Hmong-Mien languages | Origins, characteristics & dialects | Britannica. *Encyclopedia Britannica*. www.britannica.com/topic/Hmong-Mien-languages. (10 June, 2024).

Ravindranath, Maya & Abigail C. Cohn. 2014. Can a language with millions of speakers be endangered? *Journal of the Southeast Asian Linguistics Society* 7. 64–75.

Shahyd, Khalil. 2017. *Black Languages Matter: Louisiana Creole is Critically Endangered*. December 23. www.linkedin.com/pulse/black-languages-matter-louisiana-creole-critically-khalil-shahyd. (16 February, 2019).

Suraratdecha, Sumittra. 2021. Why revitalize? Benefits for communities: The case of the Black Tai community in Thailand. In *Revitalizing Endangered Languages: A Practical Guide*, 24–27. Cambridge: Cambridge University Press.

Swadesh, Morris. 1948. Sociological notes on obsolescent languages. *International Journal of American Linguistics* 14. 226–235. https://doi.org/10.1086/464009.

Tavares, Luciana Keller. 2023. The end of the world and the birth of the birds: How the Omerê Kanoé and Akuntsú survived genocide. *International Work Group for Indigenous Affairs*. www.iwgia.org/en/brazil/5223-the-end-of-the-world-and-the-birth-of-the-birds-how-the-omer%C3%AA-kano%C3%A9-and-akunts%C3%BA-survived-genocide.html. (14 June, 2024).

UNESCO. 2022. What is the international decade of indigenous languages 2022–2032. *UNESCO Indigenous Languages Decade (2022–2032)*. www.unesco.org/en/decades/indigenous-languages/about/idil2022-2032. (6 November, 2024).

UNESCO Ad Hoc Expert Group on Endangered Languages. 2003. Language vitality and endangerment. *Document Adopted by the International Expert Meeting on UNESCO Programme Safeguarding of Endangered Languages*, UNESCO. (16 June, 2024).

Wiltshire, Brandon, Steven Bird & Rebecca Hardwick. 2022. Understanding how language revitalisation works: A realist synthesis. *Journal of Multilingual and Multicultural Development*. Routledge 45(9). 1–17. https://doi.org/10.1080/01434632.2022.2134877.

Chapter 6

Language and justice

6.1 What are linguistic rights?

In Chapter 5 on language endangerment, what became quickly apparent is that not all languages share the same rights. In this chapter on language and justice, we delve further into linguistic rights and what happens when those rights are not observed.

Article 2 of the Universal Declaration of Human Rights states:

> Everyone is entitled to all the rights and freedoms set forth in this Declaration, without distinction of any kind, such as race, colour, sex, language, religion, political or other opinion, national or social origin, property, birth or other status.
>
> (United Nations 1948)

Notably, the Declaration recognises language as a possible basis of discrimination. Meant as a "common standard", the Declaration, however, has no legality and is non-binding among countries that are part of the United Nations. A much more expanded document on universal linguistics rights itself was further broached in 1996 by the International PEN Club (a worldwide association of writers) and several non-governmental organisations, which includes the following articles:

Article 10: "All language communities have equal rights."
Article 8: "All language communities are entitled to have at their disposal whatever means are necessary to ensure the transmission and continuity of their language."
Article 15: "All language communities are entitled to the official use of their language within their territory."

Article 23: "Education must help to maintain and develop the language spoken by the language community of the territory where it is provided."

Article 25: "All language communities are entitled to have at their disposal all the human and material resources necessary to ensure that their language is present to the extent they desire at all levels of education within their territory: properly trained teachers, appropriate teaching methods, textbooks, finance, buildings and equipment, traditional and innovative technology."

Article 38: "The languages and cultures of all language communities must receive equitable and non-discriminatory treatment in the communications media throughout the world."

Article 41: "All language communities have the right to use maintain and foster their language in all forms of cultural expressions. All language communities must be able to exercise this right to the full without any community's space being subjected to hegemonic occupation by a foreign culture."

(Universal Declaration of Linguistic Rights Follow-Up Committee 1998)

Unlike the Universal Declaration of Human Rights, the Universal Declaration of Linguistic Rights has never been ratified (no council or country has officially agreed to this).

Reflect on the Universal Declaration of Linguistics Rights

How much of the Universal Declaration of Linguistic Rights actually rings true regarding the language situation where you currently reside? What has to change for the Universal Declaration of Linguistic Rights to work where you live? Can you find out why it was never ratified?

It should be clear to you as you read through the previous articles that declarations represent an idealistic compass. While a lot of these rights are not met in real life, they are still worth thinking about and working towards. For example, in Canada, the right to have translation available for Cree and other indigenous languages in parliamentary debates was mooted in 2017, and such a service was actualised in 2019 (Wapachee & Wapachee 2019)—symbolising a stance reversal in Canada, where speaking indigenous languages was once heavily discouraged, where children were forced to leave their families to attend residential schools, where they were discouraged from expressing their indigenous culture, and where thousands died from poor conditions and malnourishment (Millions 2021). In 2024, in yet another move towards garnering rights for indigenous languages in Canada, the first-ever indigenous language speech in Anishininiimowin was made to the Ontario provincial legislature in Toronto. This came after an amendment was made to a previous order which required lawmakers to only use either French or English (Cecco 2024).

Positive and negative rights

Positive rights are rights that require others (usually government and institutions) to provide you with a particular resource, such as access to education and healthcare. Negative rights are rights that require others not to take away something from you, such as the right to freedom of speech. How would you classify the rights to learn through your own language in school and the rights to express yourself in your own language in parliament?

What should have become apparent is that languages themselves are not inherently powerful or less powerful, but the people and agencies who wield particular languages are, leading to situations of disrupted intergenerational transmission, language endangerment, and even discrimination based on language.

In this chapter, we go beyond looking at language endangerment to further explore the notion of justice in language use. Justice itself is a complicated multivalued concept. It encompasses the notion of fairness in the treatment of people and extends to what is morally right and upholding different sorts of rights (including social, political, moral, human, among others) but must be understood within the local context of individual societies that have their own laws and judicial systems. Here, we talk about justice where it impinges or hinges upon language, including social justice, language crimes, how language features in the legal system itself, and in some instances how language can be used to solve crimes.

6.2 What is the relationship between language, discrimination, and social justice?

Social justice deals with the fair and equitable distribution of resources and opportunities. It can be thought of as the rights to access basic services, infrastructure, and resources, as well as the ability to participate fully in economic, social, political, and cultural aspects of society without any discrimination and prejudice.

6.2.1 Linguistic profiling

Aptly, the title of a book written by John Baugh is *Linguistics in Pursuit of Justice* (2018). As a college student, the linguist worked at a laundromat, often witnessing racial discrimination on the part of the police, which piqued his interest in matters regarding linguistic diversity, racial equality, and linguistic discrimination. Today, Baugh, who is African American, is well known for his work on housing discrimination. What he noticed was that when he tried to rent apartments in affluent Palo Alto, California (home to Silicon Valley), in 1988, he would get a call back for viewing but be rejected after viewing. He realised that there must have been racial profiling going on, but because he does not sound Black over the phone, he must have avoided **linguistic profiling**. He then went on to conduct experiments—when he spoke over the phone in an African American accent or a Latino accent, his calls were not returned, or he was often told that the apartment was no longer available, as opposed to when he spoke with a "professional standard" English accent. Similar sorts of studies have since been conducted elsewhere in the world, with similar findings. For instance, in a study conducted in Bremen, Germany, in all but one district, Standard German callers received the most viewing appointments, followed by American English–accented callers, followed by Turkish callers speaking Standard English. Significantly, Turkish-accented callers had the lowest chances of getting a viewing in a more prestigious neighbourhood (Du Bois 2019). Such work in sociolinguistics can raise awareness of discrimination where it occurs. Through his work, Baugh has also gone on to give expert testimony in courts regarding whether **linguistic discrimination** has taken place, showing that linguists can play a role in ensuring social justice in these situations.

> ### A reflection exercise
>
> Reflect on an instance where you may have been the victim of linguistic discrimination or when you yourself may have unconsciously discriminated against others due to how they spoke.

Housing is not where linguistic discrimination stops. A study shows that the labour market discriminates as well based on perceived race of names. Researchers in the United States responded to help-wanted ads in Boston and Chicago newspapers by sending in fictitious résumés with randomly assigned African American– or White-sounding names. They found that names that were perceived to be White were 50 percent more likely to receive callbacks for interviews, regardless of occupation, industry, and employer size, showing that differential treatment by race still appears to be prevalent in the labour market of the United States (Bertrand & Mullainathan 2004). While this study was conducted 20 years ago, its findings are still relevant today. A more recent nationwide experiment in the United States conducted in 2024 showed that distinctive African American–sounding names reduced the probability of that the employer would actually reach out relative to White-sounding names. This study, which listed the names of the firms involved and assigned them grades based on whether discrimination was practised, showed that the firms which practised the most discrimination deal with auto services and retail. The study, which also included information on gender, showed that companies vary greatly in their treatment of women, with most having negligible preferences for gender, save for manufacturing preferring male names and apparel stores preferring female names (Kline, Rose & Walters forthcoming). The relationship between language and social justice becomes even more apparent when issues of discrimination are brought to the forefront and reported in the news. A Black man very recently filed a discrimination lawsuit against a luxury hotel in Detroit, Michigan, alleging that the hotel only responded to him with the offer of a job interview after he changed his name on his resume. He received no response with his application under his real name "Dwight Jackson", but received multiple interviews after changing his name to a more Caucasian-sounding "John Jebrowski" (Mclean 2024).

6.2.2 Discriminating with language

Language itself can be used for discrimination rather than being the basis of discrimination. A computational sociolinguistics study based in the United States using data from police body camera footage shared by the police department in Oakland, California, was conducted with the objective of examining potential racial biases in police officers' interactions with members of the public. It was established that police officers speak much less respectfully to Black than to White community members in everyday traffic stops, even after accounting for the race of the officer, the severity of infraction, the location of the stop, and its outcome. Police officers were 57 percent more likely to show respect to White interlocuters, such as through expressing apology, gratitude, and concern for one's safety. Conversely, they were 61 percent more likely to be less respectful to Black interlocutors by using phrases such as "hands on the wheel" and addressing them by their first names (Voigt et al. 2017). Findings have since been shared with police and the public to highlight the inequality in treatment, alongside recommendations.

6.2.3 More linguistic discrimination

The languages that we do not speak or that we are perceived to speak can also be used as a point of discrimination. In the United States Midwest, testimonials from members of the Spanish-speaking communities revealed a sense of disempowerment and discomfort with the social distance created by remote interpretation and a general mismatch of knowledge and expectations among interlocutors in medical interactions, which has implications for whether they get the same level of access to healthcare as dominant English speakers (Martínez et al. 2021). A different study in Catalonia showed how immigrant students experienced discriminatory practices and even racism, often reflected through a perceived lack of proficiency in Catalan and switching back to Spanish, even though these participants were educated in Catalonia (Khan & Gallego-Balsà 2021). The work, which was a collaborative effort between these students and researchers, also extended into finding ways to make others listen to this group of students. In a separate example that highlights the importance of combating workplace linguistic racism, an ethnographic study of Eastern-European immigrant women in the Australian workplace shows that these women experienced linguistic racism as a result of their non-native English language skills and marked accents—they were regularly subjected to social exclusion, mockery, mimicking, and malicious sarcasm in relation to their language use and experienced psychological trauma and distress, alongside language-based inferiority complexes (Tankosić & Dovchin 2023).

6.2.4 Combating social injustice of the language sort

So, what else can linguists do in terms of combating social injustice brought about by language? A very different sort of study shows linguists working together with language activists on revitalising the siPuthi language spoken in Lesotho, which is dominated by other languages such as Sesotho, isiXhosa, and English. It is hoped that the revitalisation of the language and the provision of materials in siPuthi, such as COVID health awareness materials, will address the inequalities in access to infrastructure, education, and healthcare to some extent, since information regarding these is scarce in the siPuthi language (Shah, Kometsi & Brenzinger 2022). In fact, one does not have to look to the developing world for these sorts of injustices and the opportunities to respond to them. During the COVID-19 outbreak when stay-at-home orders were issued in Indiana, United States, the FAQ page was published only in English. This would have affected a large group of Burmese refugees from the Chin State who speak Kuki-Chin, if not for translation timely provided by the graduate linguistics students and undergraduates at Indiana University who are part of this community (Berkson & Members of the Chin Languages Research Team 2020).

The previously mentioned studies show how linguists can be engaged with community members not just to highlight social injustice but also to address social injustice where it occurs. In Section 4, we will see another way in which linguists actively contribute to justice, through forensic linguistics.

6.3 What sort of language infractions and crimes are there?

Language infractions and crimes can involve a broad range of different actions, including the violation of censorship laws, laws against the use of particular taboo words, hate speech, racism, and even genocide denial, among others.

6.3.1 Censorship and taboo

Censorship regulates what can and cannot be said and published, because certain types of speech are perceived as being unacceptable in some way. For example, there are naming taboos and taboos regarding appropriateness. Naming taboos involve the avoidance of certain names, which is dependent on culture. In some cultures, it is taboo to use the names of people who have passed—in certain Aboriginal cultures in Australia, where people are prohibited from evoking the person's name during a set mourning period, not that this is always followed even by community members themselves (Stewart 2013). However, the usage of linguistic taboo in itself is not a language crime unless systematic laws forbid its use, and one can potentially be legally rebuked for it. For example, in ancient Japan, laws forbade utilising the personal names of rulers (Plutschow 1995). In modern times, and outside the scope of naming taboos, taboo may involve evoking what is deemed swearing or obscenity, and such an evocation can also be legally restrained. For example, Russian *mat* 'swear words', which are often associated with genitalia, are heavily used among female members of the punk subculture, and one can be fined for the use of *mat* in media and in public, where it is not permissible (Furman 2018); the most infamous or famous female group known for and jailed for using *mat* is Pussy Riot, whom you may have heard of. Beyond taboo, censorship can also involve specific topics that are deemed out of line for anyone to talk about. For example, the lèse-majesté rule in Thailand makes it illegal to defame, insult, or threaten the monarch of Thailand, the queen, heir-apparent, heir-presumptive, or regent. Arnon Nampa, a leading Thai activist, was sentenced to four years in prison in 2023 after being judged guilty over remarks he made at a rally in a case which has sparked calls for reforms of the Thai monarchy and more public debate on the role of the king (Bangkok Bureau Reuters 2023).

6.3.2 Prejudice, racism, and bigotry

Outside of censorship, language crimes can reflect prejudicial stances. In the United Kingdom, a trans woman was awarded damages after a tribunal hearing found that her employer had insisted on deadnaming her in their company system, regardless of the trans woman's reminders to the company (Tiernan 2023). Deadnaming means referring to a transgender or non-binary person by a name previously used by them before their transition and can be either unintentional or intentional, especially when one attempts to mock or deny a person's gender identity.

Racism and bigotry can also underlie language infractions and language crimes. In 2022, a man was charged and jailed in Singapore for "wounding an individual's racial feelings" (and for the possession of obscene films). Tan Boon Lee had come across an interracial couple, and as he crossed paths with them, he made the comment that it was "such a disgrace [that] an Indian man is with a Chinese girl". He accused the man of "preying on a Chinese girl" and said that a Chinese girl should not be with an Indian man (Wong 2022). In a different case, Stuart Seldowitz, a former state department employee and national security council official of the United States government, was arrested in 2023 after complaints and footage surfaced of the man's Islamophobic rants towards workers at a local halal food cart in Manhattan. In one video, Seldowitz is heard asking the vendor "Do you rape your daughter, like Mohammed did?" The vendor then chose not to engage, saying he did not speak English. Seldowitz responded by saying "That's why you're selling food in a food cart. Because you're ignorant". Seldowitz was eventually charged for aggravated harassment and several counts of stalking (Bayoumi 2023). In a different sort of bigotry, an Osijek court in Croatia sentenced four football fans to short prison terms for singing fascist songs at a football match in 2023—they sang *Ustaki se barjak vije* "The Ustasa flag flies", the Ustadas being the military arm of a fascist regime established in Croatia with the support of Nazi Germany and Italy during World War II (Tesija 2023). In newer allegations, a formal complaint has been made to the Union of European Football Associations about the Croatia and Albania fans chanting "Kill, kill, kill the Serb" during a match between Croatia and Serbia. Note that much of linguistic racism does not actually make it to the legal courts. Everyday transgressions, such as the mockery, mimicry, and malicious sarcasm used on Eastern-European women at their Australian workplaces, mentioned previously, are commonplace in many societies.

6.3.3 The propagation of falsehoods

Language infractions and crimes can be committed when falsehoods are propagated. You may be aware that in 2018 a junior association football team was rescued from a cave in Thailand. They were trapped by rising waters in the cave due to heavy rainfall and had to be rescued by divers. Before the boys were rescued, Elon Musk of Tesla Motors offered to assist the rescue mission by providing a submarine. The offer was rejected, with one of the divers, Vernon Unsworth, calling it "a PR stunt". In retaliation, Elon Musk tweeted "Sorry pedo guy, you really did ask for it". Unsworth later went on to sue Musk for defamation but was countered with what Musk said in a court filing: "'Pedo guy' was a common insult used in South Africa when I was growing up". It ensued that "pedo guy" was not used in South Africa commonly but at Musk's particular school to indicate someone who is creepy. A Los Angeles court dismissed this argument. The defence said that Unsworth failed to demonstrate any harm from the Twitter comments and even tried to profit from his role in the rescue, and in the end the jury was swayed by arguments that the tweets amounted to an offhand insult in the midst of an argument, so Musk was judged not guilty (Groom & Parsons 2019). In a different case of falsehood propagation, we see one going as far as to deny genocide, specifically the Holocaust. In 2012, Udo Pastörs, a German national, was convicted by a district court for "violating the memory of the dead and of the intentional defamation of the Jewish people". A day after Holocaust Remembrance Day, Pastörs had delivered a speech stating that the "the so-called Holocaust is being used for political and commercial purposes", and he went as far as saying that it was all a "barrage of criticism and propagandistic lies" and "Auschwitz projections". His appeal to the regional court in 2013 was dismissed as being ill founded, and a full review of his speech found that he "had used terms which amounted to denying the systematic, racially motivated, mass extermination of the Jews carried out at Auschwitz during the Third Reich" (European Court of Human Rights 2016).

6.3.4 Threats

Threats can also constitute language crimes. In the United States, a threat is legally an issue when there is a "communicated intent to inflict physical or other harm on any person or on property" and when there is a "declaration of intention or determination to inflict punishment, loss, or pain on another, or to injure another or his property by . . . some unlawful act" (Black & Nolan 1990: 1480). For example, in 2008, 65 copies of the versions of the following letter (alongside white powdery substance) were mailed to various branches of Chase Bank, the Federal Deposit Insurance Corporation, and the Office of Thrift Supervision in the United States:

> STEAL TENS OF THOUSANDS OF PEOPLE'S MONEY AND NOT EXPECTREPERCUSSIONS. IT'S PAYBACK TIME. WHAT YOU JUST BREATHED IN WILL KILL YOU WITHIN 10 DAYS. THANK JOHN SMITH AND THE FDIC FOR YOUR DEMISE.
>
> (cited in Gales 2010)

Such a threat was clearly illegal and deemed highly serious, given that the method of inflicting the threat was potentially included with the letter, even though this turned out to be a hoax (ABC News 2008). Yet, in many cases, threats are often vague, and their severity may be difficult for investigators and prosecutors to verify (Gales 2010).

This brings us to the role of forensic linguistics, a somewhat different but related area.

6.4 What is forensic linguistics?

Forensic linguistics is a specialised branch of linguistics that uses linguistics to solve issues of veracity and has a number of applications, not limited to determining authorship and assisting in crime investigations through the investigation of speech as well as writing. **Authorship attribution** has been one of the earliest applications of forensic linguistics—for example, did William Shakespeare, famous playwright, really write all the plays attributed to him? While there is no firm answer to this, a number of studies have focused on comparing the language use in his works with the writing of others, such as Francis Bacon, Henry Neville, Christophere Marlowe, and Mary Sidney, among others (Leahy 2018)—some of which considered the question of how the author might have gained knowledge of so many fields, such as law, music, astronomy, military, medicine, and others focused on textual evidence, such as their frequency of rare word usage and word couplings (such as "slings and arrows") compared to those found in Shakespeare's works (Leigh, Casson & Ewald 2019). Apart from solving mysteries in the literary world, authorship attribution in forensic linguistics is also used to investigate crime.

The case of the Unabomber

A case of where forensic linguistics was utilised successfully to establish the identity of a criminal is that of the Unabomber. Between 1978 and 1995, Theodore Kaczynski murdered three people and injured 23 in the United States with sophisticated bombs mailed to people and agencies across the country. He rejected industrialisation and modern technology, believing that these were harming the natural environment, and had mailed bombs to those he believed were responsible for these advancements. Unabomber (University and Airline Bomber) was the FBI's case identifier before Kaczynski's identity was unveiled. Crucially, Kaczynski had mailed several letters as well as a "manifesto" to media outlets, saying that he would desist if his demands to abandon modern advances were met. Comparisons of the typewritten manifesto with essays that Kaczynski had sent to his brother were made, and similarities in writing led investigators to determine that he was the Unabomber, leading to his capture and subsequent incarceration (Ray 2024).

Thus, we see an example of forensic linguistics that demonstrates some of the central issues such as whether it was plausible that this was a person who would write a certain thing or if it might be the same person who wrote two things. Of course, such investigations extend to voice as well, such as whether a suspect's voice can indeed be identified from amongst other voices, and so on. So how does sociolinguistics feature directly in this? A good example that demonstrates how sociolinguistics features in forensic linguistics is the infamous case of the Yorkshire Ripper, who murdered at least 13 women between 1975 and 1980 in West Yorkshire, England.

The case of the Yorkshire Ripper

In 1979, a tape and letters were received by the police, purportedly having been sent by the Yorkshire Ripper. The accent on the tape led the police to believe that the Yorkshire Ripper did not have a Yorkshire accent, leading authorities to focus on the Castletown area and discontinue focusing on suspects in Yorkshire, despite some survivors telling the police that the perpetrator had a Yorkshire accent. Some forensic phoneticians (who focus on speech sounds) had analysed the tape and determined that the speaker had an accent typical of the Castletown area of Wearside, and the assailant was hence dubbed Wearside Jack. Others, however, felt that the tape was a hoax, given that the speaker's accent located the speaker as having grown up far away from where the crimes took place, and that the speaker's voice had distinctive features that would have made him easily identifiable—these linguists felt that the actual perpetrator would have tried a whole lot harder to disguise his voice. It was unfortunate, then, that the police believed in the authenticity of the letters and tape, because they turned out to be a hoax. In the meantime, the actual Yorkshire Ripper had murdered another three additional victims. The other issue with the investigation was that while sex workers had been targeted at the start, the Yorkshire Ripper had begun targeting non-sex workers as well, but the police were adamant that the Yorkshire Ripper only targeted sex workers and dismissed victims who did not fit this profile—so the testimony of one such victim was ignored completely, as well as the accurate sketch that she aided in creating. Peter Sutcliffe, the Yorkshire Ripper, was finally arrested in Sheffield when police spotted his fake license plates and took him into custody, and he confessed to his crimes during interrogation. At

> the trial, Sutcliffe himself said, "It was a miracle they did not apprehend me earlier—they had all the facts" (Picotti 2023). In 2005, using DNA tests on the material sent in by the hoaxer, the police found a match in the United Kingdom DNA Database with samples obtained from John Humble for drunken and disorderly behaviour, and he was sentenced to eight years in prison for his hoax (Herbert 2006).

While there were a couple of things that went wrong with the investigation, we can see how sociolinguistics, in particular regional dialect variation, may play a crucial role in investigations.

6.5 So how does language feature in the legal system?

The study of language use within the legal system is also an interesting field. As you might expect, language used in law statutes and legal documents (some call this 'legalese') can be confusing for most members of the public. The judiciary system relies on precise wording of these texts to interpret laws and transgressions, which makes it all the more important that these documents be accessible to those who speak a different language or have limited literacy.

Predictably, legal contracts themselves can be a cause of disputes. The most infamous case perhaps is the "hairy hand" case (Fuller 2006).

The case of the hairy hand

In 1915, George A. Hawkins' hand was scarred after contact with an electrical wire from turning on a light in his family home's kitchen (this was 1915, after all!). His father was approached by a local doctor in their state of New Hampshire. Dr. Edward McGee guaranteed to make the injured hand a "one hundred percent good hand", and he utilised a method of skin grafting, with skin from Hawkins' chest area, which resulted in the palm of Hawkin's hand growing thick hair. Hawkins sued McGee for breach of contract in 1926 for receiving a hairy

> hand instead of a "one hundred percent good hand", as well as for the pain from the operation. The legal language used in the contract, as well as terms such as "guaranteed" and "success", were contested in a legal battle. In the end, the New Hampshire supreme court awarded him damages on the basis of what was promised on the contract (the "one hundred percent good hand") but dismissed any claims for pain and suffering, because pain and suffering were deemed to be understood and unspoken outcomes from a surgery.

Today, the field that explores how legal language is used and how it impacts legal processes and interpretations, and the practice of law is known as '**jurilinguistics**' in some parts of the world. At the time of writing, the only place that employs jurilinguists is Canada. These jurilinguists are meant to review translations of decisions from the courts, but notably, they are meant to translate between English and French, which leads to questions about what happens if someone in need of legal help does not speak either of these languages. Unsurprisingly, there is very little parity in access to legal services and justice globally, particularly if one does not speak the dominant language of that place (see Section 2 on language and social justice).

6.5.1 Language as a source of contention in legal proceedings

Separately, language can be a source of contention in legal proceedings itself. Warren Demesme was arrested for raping a juvenile in Louisiana. During his interrogation, he reportedly said:

> This is how I feel, if y'all think I did it, I know that I didn't do it so why don't you just give me a **lawyer dog** 'cause this is not what's up.
> (Jackman 2017, emphasis mine)

Was it clear that he was asking for a lawyer, with the term "dog" being commonly used in vernacular speech, such as "what's up dog?", or did he in fact ask for a "lawyer dog"? Demesme had repeatedly denied the crime and was possibly getting frustrated. But instead of invoking his right to an attorney, he was denied one and the police did not stop their questioning (if the suspect had asked for a lawyer, they would have been legally obliged to stop questioning the suspect, as bound by the Miranda rights in the United States court of law; more on that later). The courts in Louisiana claimed that they did not think he was asking for a lawyer but a canine attorney, which does not exist and would not cause the police to stop their questioning. In the end, Demesme was found guilty of aggravated rape and indecent behaviour with a juvenile (Jackman 2017).

6.5.2 Linguistic discrimination in legal proceedings

Language can also be a source of discrimination within the legal system. Rachel Jeantel was the leading prosecution witness when White police officer George Zimmerman was tried for killing an unarmed Black teenager, Trayvon Martin, in 2012. Jeantel, who was Martin's friend, had spoken to him shortly before the shooting and would have provided important perspective on Martin's state of mind leading up to the incident. She spoke in African American Vernacular English, and her testimony was dismissed as being incomprehensible and therefore not credible to a mostly White courtroom. Linguistic analysis by sociolinguists John Rickford and Sharese King showed that Rachel Jeantel spoke a highly systematic African American Vernacular English, with possible Caribbean influence (Rickford & King 2016). For example, her statements in her deposition showed the use of *bin* as remote phase marker as well as the invariant habitual *be*:

> I **BIN** knew I was the last person to talk to Trayvon. (= 'had known for a long time').
>
> That's where his headset **be** at.
>
> Sometimes my friends **be** texting for me, when I'm busy.
> (Rickford & King 2016: 958, emphasis theirs)

Nothing in the way in which Rachel Jeantel provided her deposition showed that she was an unreliable witness. Unfamiliarity with African American Vernacular English as well as institutionalised racism, however, led to her crucial testimony being dismissed. In the end,

Zimmerman was acquitted of all charges, the jury deciding that he had acted in self-defence. Widespread protests ensued and, in the aftermath, hopefully, broader dialogues on racial profiling and legal justice will continue happening.

6.5.3 Parity in the legal system

Parity, or the concept of equality and fairness, is also important for forensic linguistics when it comes to ensuring the rights of those undergoing legal proceedings. In the United States courts, for instance, there is what is known as Miranda rights. Before interrogation, suspects must be told that they have the right to remain silent; that anything they say can be used against them in court; that they have the right to an attorney; and that if they cannot afford an attorney, one will be provided for them. One of the applications of forensic linguistics is an examination of police and court proceedings to ensure that the rights of everyone, including suspects, are respected.

Miranda and his rights

Miranda rights themselves came about when Ernesto Miranda, a 24-year-old man, was accused of kidnapping, raping, and robbing a woman in Arizona in 1963. Miranda wrote a confession to the kidnapping and rape of the woman on sheets of paper that had these lines printed at the top: "this statement has been made voluntarily and of my own free will, with no threats, coercion or promises of immunity and with full knowledge of my legal rights, understanding any statement that I make can and will be used against me". This confession was admitted to court as sole evidence, but Miranda's lawyer argued that Miranda was not informed of his right to have an attorney present or of his right to stay silent at arrest and during his interrogation. His conviction was not overturned. But the case made it as far as the United States Supreme Court (its highest court), which gave rise to the Miranda warning, which states that the suspect has the right to remain silent, that anything they say can be used against them

> in a court of law, that the suspect has the right to an attorney, that an attorney will be provided for them if they are not able to afford one, and that the suspect has the right to either answer questions without an attorney present or stop answering at any time until they talk to an attorney (Levesque 2006).

While the Miranda rights are specific to the United States, other countries have their own versions of similar rights, such as the Interrogation Caution in Japan that informs suspects of their rights to remain silent and have a lawyer present. Part of forensic linguistics deals with whether such warnings are clearly and effectively communicated and whether there were any issues with language use that may have affected the validity of a confession or statement. This brings us to the role of transcription.

6.6 What is the role of transcription?

Transcription is a much harder endeavour than one might expect. **Transcription** aims to provide an accurate written record of what is said, and a good transcript gives us information about how something was said as well. Surprisingly or otherwise, transcription of a police interrogation or a legal proceeding may be highly consequential for the outcome of a trial. Transcription in English itself is surprisingly complicated, and transcription in a different language is a whole other tall order altogether.

6.6.1 The complications of transcribing

Even in English, transcription is an inherently complicated task, made even more complicated by the variety of English that the transcriber is familiar with and their own agenda or stance. The following are two versions of a police interrogation that appear in Bucholtz (2000). Mary Bucholtz, a prominent sociolinguist working in the field of discourse, had been involved as a pro bono consultant in a criminal case in California in 1995 at the request of the public defender of the case. Interrogation had led to a confession of burglary, but the defendant's lawyer believed that the confession had been coerced and that the defendant's rights to remain silent (Miranda rights in the United States court of law) had been disregarded. Compare the two versions of the same police interrogation (transcripts from Bucholtz 2000).

Police transcript
Q=Police officer. A=Client

1. A. I'll tell you every—every single thing.
2. Q. Okay.
3. A. U mean what—*see you got to understand*
4. (unintelligible).

5. Q. (Unintelligible.)

6. A. Yeah.

7. Q. Yeah, you've got to understand (unintelligible) house?

8. A. Yeah.
9. Q. Okay. You've got to understand. I'm not going to *make you deal* with anybody—

10. A. Well, I don't want to—
11. Q.—unless—unless I know what *I'm doing*. You know what I'm saying?
...
12. Q. What's the (unintelligible)?

13. A. *(Unintelligible.)*

14. Q. What are you going to ask me to do?
15. A. I want to give her a kiss.
16. Q. I'll do that for you. (Unintelligible.)
17. A. Huh?
18. Q. You've got my word.
19. A. I've got your word?
20. Q. You've got my word.

Researcher transcript
Pol=Police officer. Cli=Client

1. Cli: I'll tell you every—every single thing.
2. Pol: Okay.
3. Cli: I mean what—

4. *Pol: See you got to understand*
5. (unintelligible).
6. *Cli:* Do me a favor, man, that's it.
7. *Pol: Yeah?*
8. Cli: Yeah.
9. Pol: Okay. You've got to understand (unintelli-gible).
10. Cli: Yeah.
11. Pol: Okay. You've got to understand, I'm not going to *make a deal* with anybody—
12. Cli: Well, I don't want to—
13. Pol—unless—unless I know what *I'm deal-ing with*. You know what I'm saying?
...
14. *Pol: Now are we going to talk about it? The other part?*
15. *Cli: What are you guys going to do for me? Take care of what I ask you to do for me.*
16. Pol: What are you going to ask me to do?
17. Cli: I want to give her a kiss.
18. Pol: I'll do that for you.
19. Cli: Promise?
20. *Pol: Not before* we talk.
21. Cli: Huh?
22. Pol: You've got my word.
23. Cli: I've got your word?
24. Pol: You've got my word.

Language and justice 141

If you have taken some time to compare the two transcripts, you will see that by representing certain exchanges as 'unintelligible' and misattributing other utterances, the coercion of confession which showed the police officer taking advantage of the defendant's vulnerable emotional state is erased. In this particular case, even though the defendant's lawyer argued that the officer's behaviour had a coercive effect on the defendant, and a revised transcript was submitted to court, the client was still convicted of burglary, where the district attorney's argument that confession was freely given still succeeded. Regardless, you can see how important accurate transcripts are for the interpretation of what has happened and, ultimately and hopefully, in judgements.

6.6.2 The complications of transcribing in a different variety

Complexities further ensue, as we have seen in Rachel Jeantel's experience, when a different variety of English is encountered. In an important piece of research conducted in Philadelphia, Pennsylvania, the accuracy of court reporters at transcribing African American Vernacular English was tested (Jones et al. 2019). Court reporters are required to be certified at 95 percent accuracy for transcription, but such certification is based primarily on the speech of lawyers and judges (who clearly would speak Standard English in courts rather than other vernacular forms). Nine native speakers of African American Vernacular English were recorded reading 83 sentences, all of which taken from actual speech. Some examples of sentences included "When you tryna go to the store?" and "Don't nobody never say nothing to them", among others. As expected, the court reporters transcribed only 59.5 percent of the sentences accurately. Thirty-one percent of the sentences had transcription errors that changed the 'who', 'what', 'when', or 'where' of the sentences, which can have real-life repercussions had these utterances been part of an actual testimony or deposition. Judgements ultimately get passed based on what is said, and the results from this study show how a lot more needs to be done in terms of getting accurate transcriptions of nonstandard English speakers.

The problem of accurately representing what is said is not a problem unique to the United States. The following comes from the testimony of a Jamaican Creole speaker testifying in a police interview in the United Kingdom (Brown-Blake & Chambers 2008). What he actually said can be compared to what was mistranscribed:

Accurately transcribed utterance:

wen	mi	ier	di	bap	bap,		mi	drap
when	I	heard	the	bap	bap [the shots],		I	fell

a	**groun**	an	den	mi	staat	ron
to.the	ground	and	then	I	started.to	run.

Mistranscribed utterance:

> When I heard the shot (bap, bap), I **drop the gun**, and then I run.
> (cited in Brown-Blake & Chambers 2008)

When you compare both, you realise how much more incriminating the mistranscribed utterance is. *Drop* in the mistranscribed utterance has been interpreted as a transitive verb (requiring that something is dropped), rather than 'to fall', as it is used in Jamaican Creole. In Jamaican Creole, *a* indicates the preposition 'to', rather than the indefinite article. You can also see how the phonetically similar *groun* (GRONG) in Jamaican Creole has been misinterpreted as 'gun'. Unsurprisingly, the mistranscription was carried out by a person familiar with Standard English but not with Jamaican Creole (and perhaps with a certain amount of racial profiling involved). Thankfully, the transcription was checked against the audio recording of the testimony by Paul Chambers, a Jamaican Creole interpreter (Brown-Blake & Chambers 2008). Otherwise, legal consequences would have been dire.

6.6.3 The complications of transcribing in a different language

Where other languages are concerned, transcription or even the ability to provide a transcript in the language becomes even more problematic. A case in Singapore in 1972 centred on the inability to provide a transcript in the original language—in this case, Hokkien. An opposition political party alleged that a member of the ruling party had committed slander, because he had claimed that the opposition party had accepted money inappropriately from Malaysia. The party sued the speaker for slander. The speech in which the slander was alleged was given in Hokkien, translated into Singapore's four official languages (English, Mandarin, Malay, and Tamil), and broadcast in these languages over national television. The issue of transcription arose, however, because the original speech had been made in Hokkien, a Sinitic Southern Min language that isn't Mandarin. Even though the speech had been translated and broadcast in Singapore's four official languages, the opposition party was unable to obtain a transcript of what was originally said (Lydgate 2015). The High Court in Singapore dismissed the case, stating that transcript in the original language had not been provided and that if slander had been alleged in a language other than English, it must be set out in the statement of claim in that language and accompanied with a literal translation in that language (Singapore High Court 1974).

The importance of transcription in legal proceedings lies in maintaining an accurate, fair, and transparent legal process. The importance of transcription, which might seem like a boring topic and a tedious task altogether, cannot be overstated. As you can see from the examples in this section, accurate transcriptions help uphold the integrity of the system of justice itself and are an important part of ensuring justice and social justice for speakers of different varieties of languages or different languages altogether.

References

ABC News. 2008. Chase bank hoax threat letters sent from Amarillo, Texas. *ABC News*. https://abcnews.go.com/Blotter/story?id=6082535&page=1. (22 July, 2024).

Bangkok Bureau Reuters. 2023. Lawyer who called for Thai monarchy reforms sentenced to 4 years for royal insults. *Reuters*. Bangkok, sec. Asia Pacific. www.reuters.com/world/asia-pacific/activist-who-called-thai-monarchy-reforms-sentenced-four-years-royal-insults-2023-09-26/. (10 July, 2024).

Baugh, John. 2018. *Linguistics in Pursuit of Justice*. Cambridge: Cambridge University Press. https://doi.org/10.1017/9781316597750.

Bayoumi, Moustafa. 2023. Stuart Seldowitz's hateful behavior is US foreign policy unmasked. *The Guardian*, sec. Opinion. www.theguardian.com/commentisfree/2023/nov/28/stuart-seldowitz-islamophobia-us-diplomat. (17 July, 2024).

Berkson, Kelly H. & Members of the Chin Languages Research Team. 2020. *COVID-19 Informational Materials in Hakha Lai.* www.chinlanguages.org.

Bertrand, Marianne & Sendhil Mullainathan. 2004. Are Emily and Greg more employable than Lakisha and Jamal? A field experiment on labor market discrimination. *American Economic Review* 94(4). 991–1013. https://doi.org/10.1257/0002828042002561.

Black, Henry Campbell & Joseph R. Nolan. 1990. *Black's Law Dictionary.* 6th edition. St. Paul, MN: West Publishing Company.

Brown-Blake, Celia Nadine & Paul Chambers. 2008. The Jamaican Creole speaker in the UK justice system. *International Journal of Speech, Language and the Law* 14(2). 269–294. https://doi.org/10.1558/ijsll.v14i2.269.

Bucholtz, Mary. 2000. The politics of transcription. *Journal of Pragmatics* 32.

Cecco, Leyland. 2024. In historic first, Canada lawmaker addresses legislature in Indigenous language. *The Guardian*, sec. World news. www.theguardian.com/world/article/2024/may/28/canada-solmamakwa-speech-first-nation-language. (18 July, 2024).

Du Bois, Inke. 2019. Linguistic discrimination across neighbourhoods: Turkish, US-American and German names and accents in urban apartment search. *Journal of Language and Discrimination* 3(2). 92–119. https://doi.org/10.1558/jld.39973.

European Court of Human Rights. 2016. *Pastörs v. Germany (Communicated).* https://hudoc.echr.coe.int/eng?i=001-166885. (17 July, 2024).

Fuller, Lon L. 2006. *Basic Contract Law.* St. Paul, MN: Thomson/West. http://archive.org/details/basiccontractlaw0000full. (30 July, 2024).

Furman, Michael Douglas. 2018. Of mat and men: Taboo words and the language of Russian female punks. *Laboratorium: Russian Review of Social Research* 10(1). 5–28.

Gales, Tammy Angela. 2010. *Ideologies of Violence: A Corpus and Discourse Analytic Approach to Stance in Threatening Communications.* California: University of California Davis PhD dissertation.

Groom, Nichola & Rachel Parsons. 2019. Tesla boss Elon Musk wins defamation trial over his "pedo guy" tweet. *Reuters*, sec. Technology. www.reuters.com/article/technology/tesla-boss-elonmusk-wins-defamation-trial-over-his-pedo-guy-tweet-idUS KBN1YA13S/. (18 July, 2024).

Herbert, Ian. 2006. Wearside Jack: I deserve to go to jail for "evil" Ripper hoax. *The Independent*, sec. News. www.independent.co.uk/news/uk/crime/wearside-jack-i-deserve-to-go-to-jail-for-evil-ripper-hoax-6106028.html. (19 July, 2024).

Jackman, Tom. 2017. The suspect told police "give me a lawyer dog": The court says he wasn't asking for a lawyer. *Washington Post*. www.washingtonpost.com/news/true-crime/wp/2017/11/02/the-suspect-told-police-give-me-a-lawyer-dog-the-court-says-he-wasnt-asking-for-a-lawyer/. (30 July, 2024).

Jones, Taylor, Jessica Rose Kalbfeld, Ryan Hancock & Robin Clark. 2019. Testifying while black: An experimental study of court reporter accuracy in transcription of African American English. *Language*. Linguistic Society of America 95(2). e216–e252.

Khan, Kamran & LíDIA Gallego-Balsà. 2021. Racialized trajectories to Catalan higher education: Language, anti-racism and the "politics of listening." *Applied Linguistics* 42(6). 1083–1096. https://doi.org/10.1093/applin/amab055.

Kline, Patrick M., Evan K. Rose & Christopher R. Walters. forthcoming. A discrimination report card. *American Economic Review*.

Leahy, William D. Professor (ed.). 2018. *My Shakespeare: The Authorship Controversy: Experts Examine the Arguments for Bacon, Neville, Oxford, Marlowe, Mary Sidney, Shakspere, and Shakespeare*. Edward Everett Root.

Leigh, R. John, John Casson & David Ewald. 2019. A scientific approach to the Shakespeare authorship question. *Sage Open*. SAGE Publications 9(1). 2158244018823465. https://doi.org/10.1177/2158244018823465.

Levesque, Roger J. R. 2006. *The Psychology and Law of Criminal Justice Processes*. Nova Publishers.

Lydgate, Chris. 2015. I thought that dawn had come to the political landscape of Singapore. *Inside Story*. https://insidestory.org.au/i-thought-that-dawn-had-come-to-the-political-landscape-of-singapore/. (28 July, 2024).

Martínez, Glenn A., Rachel E. Showstack, Dalia Magaña, Parizad Dejbord-Sawan & Karol J. Hardin. 2021. Pursuing testimonial justice: Language access through patient-centered outcomes research with Spanish speakers. *Applied Linguistics* 42(6). 1110–1124. https://doi.org/10.1093/applin/amab060.

Mclean, Nia. 2024. A Black man got a job interview after he changed the name on his resume: Now, he's suing for discrimination. *CNN*. www.cnn.com/2024/07/10/us/dwight-jackson-employment-discrimination-lawsuit-reaj/index.html. (16 July, 2024).

Millions, Ian Mosby, Erin. 2021. Canada's residential schools were a horror. *Scientific American*. www.scientificamerican.com/article/canadas-residential-schools-were-a-horror/. (18 July, 2024).

Picotti, Tyler. 2023. "Yorkshire Ripper" peter sutcliffe is featured in a new true crime miniseries. *Biography*. www.biography.com/crime/peter-sutcliffe. (19 July, 2024).

Plutschow, Herbert E. 1995. *Japan's Name Culture: The Significance of Names in a Religious, Political and Social Context*. Kent, UK: Japan Library.

Ray, Michael. 2024. Ted Kaczynski | biography, manifesto, & UNABOM case | Britannica. *Britannica*. www.britannica.com/biography/Ted-Kaczynski. (22 July, 2024).

Rickford, John R. & Sharese King. 2016. Language and linguistics on trial: Hearing Rachel Jeantel (and other vernacular speakers) in the courtroom and beyond. *Language* 92(4). 948–988. https://doi.org/10.1353/lan.2016.0078.

Shah, Sheena, Letzadzo Kometsi & Matthias Brenzinger. 2022. Language activists and linguists in pursuit of the siPhuthi cause. *Annual Review of Applied Linguistics* 42. 93–101. https://doi.org/10.1017/S0267190522000058.

Singapore High Court. 1974. Worker's party v Tay Boon Too. *Singapore Law Reports (Reissue)* 204.

Stewart, Cameron. 2013. Naming taboo often ignored in breaking news. *The Weekend Australian*. Sydney.

Tankosić, Ana & Sender Dovchin. 2023. (C)overt linguistic racism: Eastern-European background immigrant women in the Australian workplace. *Ethnicities*. SAGE Publications 23(5). 726–757. https://doi.org/10.1177/14687968211005104.

Tesija, Vuk. 2023. Croatia court jails football fans for chanting fascist song. *BalkanInsight*. https://balkaninsight.com/2023/10/16/croatia-court-jails-football-fans-for-chanting-fascist-song/. (17 July, 2024).

Tiernan, Han. 2023. Trans woman awarded £25,000 in case against employer who deadnamed her. *Yahoo News*. https://uk.news.yahoo.com/trans-woman-awarded-25-000-135724336.html. (10 July, 2024).

United Nations. 1948. *Universal Declaration of Human Rights*. United Nations. www.un.org/en/about-us/universal-declaration-of-human-rights. (1 July, 2024).

Universal Declaration of Linguistic Rights Follow-Up Committee. 1998. *Universal Declarations of Linguistic Rights*. Barcelona: Institut d'Edicions de la Diputació de Barcelona. https://culturalrights.net/descargas/drets_culturals389.pdf. (29 June, 2023).

Voigt, Rob, Nicholas P. Camp, Vinodkumar Prabhakaran, William L. Hamilton, Rebecca C. Hetey, Camilla M. Griffiths, David Jurgens, Dan Jurafsky & Jennifer L. Eberhardt. 2017. Language from police body camera footage shows racial disparities in officer respect. *Proceedings of the National Academy of Sciences*. Proceedings of the National Academy of Sciences 114(25). 6521–6526. https://doi.org/10.1073/pnas.1702413114.

Wapachee, Celina & Cheryl Wapachee. 2019. Cree translator in house of commons "proud" to be part of history. *CBC News*. www.cbc.ca/news/canada/north/translator-house-of-commons-1.5016715. (18 July, 2024).

Wong, Shiying. 2022. Ex-Ngee Ann Poly lecturer jailed, trial reveals his daughter had left home with an Indian boyfriend. *AsiaOne*. Singapore, sec. Singapore. www.asiaone.com/singapore/angry-employer-prints-100-leaflets-shaming-maid-who-borrowed-2000-and-went-mia-after-dads. (17 July, 2024).

Chapter 7

Language and computing

We are at an exciting inflection point in history, where we get to experience first-hand technological disruptions that will change the way humans interact with technology. Just as with the advent of the Internet, the growth of generative AI and large language models like ChatGPT is changing the way we do things. **Large language models (LLMs)** are advanced artificial intelligence systems designed to process, generate, and interact with human language in sophisticated ways. Notice that I have used the word "process" instead of "understand", because whether we are already at the stage of having computers *understand* human language may still be up for debate.

7.1 Do computers understand language?

When you tell Siri to play you a certain song, and it plays you that song, do you say that the Apple device that is executing Siri has an understanding of language? When you ask Amazon's Alexa about the weather, and Alexa tells you that it is 30 degrees Celsius out today, sunny, with a slight chance of rain, would you say that Alexa understands language? Similarly, when you ask ChatGPT if it can make an email you want to send to your boss sound a lot more polite, and it does so for you, does it mean that the computer running ChatGPT possesses some consciousness of how language works? The question of whether computers understand language has become more valid than ever, now that machines are so advanced that you sometimes wonder if you are talking to a bot or a human. In fact, in the face of malicious actors using increasingly capable technology for fraud, cyberattacks, and disinformation campaigns, a group of technological industry people and academics (including individuals from OpenAI and Microsoft) have banded together to propose that technologists and policymakers develop more novel ways of verifying humanhood without impinging on their privacy or anonymity, such as a system of encrypted "personhood credentials" which humans can receive when they prove their personhood offline that they can then use to log in for various online services (Oremus 2024). This is how far we have come. Technology has come a long way since the time of Colossus—one of the very first electronic digital computers used by British codebreakers to decipher encrypted German messages in World War II. However, to better understand what it means for a computer to understand language, it might be good to leave the most modern technology aside for now and travel back in time for a bit.

7.1.1 The Turing test

As early as the 1950s, British mathematician, computer scientist, and philosopher Alan Turing came up with an idea of a test that is now known as the **Turing test**. He wanted to know if machines could think. In the typical version of his test, a human judge interacts with both a human and a machine through text. The human judge is not able to see their interlocutor, and based on the responses produced by their interlocutor, the human must determine which of the two is human and which is machine. In its original formulation, if at least 30 percent of the human judges are not able to reliably distinguish machine from human based on these responses, then one can say that the machine has passed the Turing test and that the machine is "thinking" (Turing 1950). Notably, computers and the programs that they run have become more and more sophisticated. In 2014, Eugene Goostman, a chatbot that was trying to pass as a 13-year-old boy from Odessa in Ukraine, officially passed the Turing test conducted by the Royal Society in London with 33 percent of the human judges thinking that he was human (Aamoth 2014). There have, however, been detractors who have questioned the validity of the test, saying that if you observe Goostman's responses closely enough, you would be able to tell that he isn't human. A decade later, you might ask if much more advanced large language models like ChatGPT can pass the Turing test. It might seem that ChatGPT can generate responses that are very human-like and relevant, but if you test it for long enough, you may begin to see it struggle to still sound human while keeping up with the conversation. If trained on enough data on a specific topic, ChatGPT can get extremely specific, but if lacking such training data on a specific topic, it can be too vague and general to pass off as human. Additionally, while ChatGPT imitates human conversations, some might say it lacks true human understanding. This brings us to the Chinese room problem.

7.1.2 A thought experiment: the Chinese room problem

The **Chinese room problem** is a thought experiment envisioned by John Searle, an American philosopher. The Chinese room problem was proposed because John Searle did not think that passing the Turing test was enough to say that a machine possess true understanding of language or even consciousness. In the Chinese room problem, you have a person who does not speak or understand Chinese in the room. What this person has, however, is access to a large set of Chinese symbols and instructions for manipulating these symbols—in other words, some sort of rulebook. A person outside of the room writes questions in Chinese and slips them under the door of the Chinese room, and, using the rulebook, the person in the Chinese room can match the symbols, figure out what is being said, and respond appropriately using the set of symbols and the rules provided. The question that is asked, then, is whether the person inside the room actually understands Chinese. This is a valid question, since it might seem to the person outside the room that their interlocutor does—the person outside the room receives responses that appear entirely adequate, as if they came from someone who understands Chinese. Searle states that the person inside the room does not actually understand the language and that they are simply following a set of rules to manipulate symbols, without an actual understanding of what is being said. In relation to this, we can ask if a machine running a program is simply responding to us by putting together symbols and rules provided in a rulebook, regardless of how convincing its response is, and if the machine has true understanding of language. You would most likely not say that the person in the Chinese room understands Chinese. So, would you say that a machine that responds to Chinese or to any other language has an understanding of that language (Searle 1980)?

> **How human are they?**
>
> Out of all the virtual assistants and artificial intelligence systems (e.g. Siri, Alexa, Google Assistant, ChatGPT, etc.) that you have come across and operated, which one seems most human to you? What is the basis of your evaluation?

7.1.3 Yet another thought experiment: the octopus test

An even more novel but no less interesting way to think about whether computers indeed understand language is the **octopus test** proposed by computational linguists Emily Bender and Alexander Koller. In this thought experiment, A and B are two fluent speakers of the same language who are stranded on two separate, uninhabited islands. They somehow have the ability to use telegraphs to send messages to each other via an underwater cable (presumably the previous inhabitants have left these behind). O is a "hyper-intelligent deep-sea octopus" who cannot observe first-hand what is happening on the islands, but he is able to somehow access A and B's conversations by tapping in on the underwater cable. O is also excellent at detecting statistic patterns, and he has worked out how B will most likely respond to A's utterance. O has also learnt that some words can be used in place of others. What O does not know, however, is what objects these words refer to in the real world (the real-world referents). There are three other parts to this thought experiment. In the first part of it, O has become lonely and pretends to be B as he intercepts A's messages and responds to A—is he able to deceive A? The degree to which A can be deceived depends on what topics they are engaged in. To A, O comes across as B convincingly, as long as the conversation is limited to simple everyday conversation that does not relate to anything in the actual world since O has never seen A and B's worlds and does not know how words map onto things in real life. In the second part of the thought experiment, A has invented a coconut catapult and sends instructions on building said catapult to B, asking for B's input. O taps into the message but cannot actually build anything with these instructions, because he clearly does not know what words such as "coconut" refer to. O can respond with "Cool idea, great job!" because it is what B would say when A talks about "ropes and nails". O neither understands the coconut catapult building instruction, nor does he understand his own response. In the third part of this thought experiment, A faces an angry bear and asks B if B has any ideas about building a weapon that would ward off the angry bear. A has some sticks that could possibly be used. Unsurprisingly, sticks or no sticks, O clearly cannot help A solve her dilemma, since he cannot map words onto things in the real world, and he is unable to think creatively as well. At this point, as Bender and Koller puts it, he would have well and truly failed the Turing test if A hasn't already been eaten by the bear (Bender & Koller 2020). The thought experiment put forth here supposedly shows the limitations of a machine's understanding and at the same time demonstrates the importance of a listener's role in understanding the communication. At the points where A understood what was produced by O, it was not because O had the goal to convey information but because A had attributed these messages to B and could make sense of the messages in this particular context. Think of A perhaps as you, the end user of whatever AI system it is that you are using to generate a recipe for buttermilk pancakes or a backpacker's itinerary of Europe. Does the AI really know what "buttermilk" tastes like or what it means to have an "experience"? And we don't mean if it can generate the literal meanings of these words or the contexts they usually appear in, because we know it can.

7.2 Introducing natural language processing and/or understanding

The three previous thought experiments are all slightly different in nature, but when you compare the Turing test with the Chinese room problem or the earlier bits of the octopus test with the later bits of the octopus test, it becomes apparent that there is a difference between the abilities to process language versus understanding it. This key difference fundamentally underlies the overall purported aims of natural language processing and natural language understanding. Natural language processing as a whole is slightly more developed than what some think of its subfield, so let us focus on that first.

7.2.1 What is natural language processing?

Natural language processing (NLP) seems current but has its underpinnings in early computational linguistics. A lot of early work focused on simple language processing models and **machine translation** using a more rule-based system, not unlike what has been depicted in the Chinese room problem. Explicit rules are fed to the machine for the computer and/or program to do simple things, such as **machine translation, speech recognition** (converting spoken language into text), and even **identifying and extracting information**, like grammatical categories (such as identifying whether something is a noun or a verb). As long as the rule exists in the "rulebook", whether it be a grammatical rule for machine translation or a phonological rule for speech recognition, the computer would be able to handle processing for language patterns that fall within the confines of that rule. You might already guess the major issue that might arise from something like this—these systems are not able to parse language input when the input is not covered by these rules. This is also where sociolinguistics comes in as well, and you should be well aware of this by now—people vary in the way that they speak due to sociolinguistic reasons (gender, age, affiliation, region, etc.) in addition to reasons of idiosyncrasy. Unless one had expertise in the different regional dialects that exist, as well as all the time and resources to go in to enter all these other rules into the system, you can see that the system is going to be somewhat simplistic and limited in terms of what it can do.

One of the most famous early rule-based systems that is commonly cited in NLP literature is ELIZA, which was created by Joseph Weizenbaum in 1966. ELIZA was developed to simulate conversations as though you were talking to a psychotherapist. It utilised pattern matching, which is often used in conjunction with rule-based models to recognise key phrases or words in the input of the user (not unlike the person in the Chinese room who is matching what they receive with the symbols and rules that they are equipped with) and applied rules to generate responses in the style of a psychotherapist. While ELIZA was rather simple in terms of what it could handle and was critiqued as lacking true understanding, it was at that time seminal as an early exploration of communication between humans and machines. In fact, Weizenbaum himself was taken aback when he learnt that some people, his secretary included, began attributing human-like feelings to ELIZA and forming attachments with it (1976) (more on human-computer interactions later)!

> **Try out ELIZA**
>
> You are likely to be able to find a few versions of ELIZA online. Try talking to one. Does it feel like a real human being? Are there conversation topics that it is better at? Remember it is meant to simulate talking to a psychotherapist! Are there topics that it is much worse at, and what are these topics?

Later developments in NLP meant that, for a while, computational linguists moved on from rule-based systems to statistical methods for analysing and modelling the human language. The statistical-based systems involved feeding the system large amounts of textual data (written and/or spoken), so that patterns and relations in the language are learned through observing actual linguistic input (and not through rules). The actual algorithms that are used for learning from these large datasets can differ. But based on what the system has learnt from this input, the machine is able to make predictions regarding the likelihood of different outcomes based on what it is asked to do. Like rule-based systems, statistical systems can also be used for machine translation, speech recognition, and assigning grammatical categories, among others. These statistical-based models are often better at handling variability in the way people talk or write, since they do not rely on rigid rules. They are also more easily scalable. Instead of thinking up all the possible rules that are missing from the rulebook, those who operate a statistical-based model simply have to feed the model more data from the domains that are lacking (such as texts and/or recordings from less-represented regions or dialects around the world). As you might expect, statistical methods only became possible when more and more textual data became readily available and computers became much more capable in terms of their processing capacities. One of the most well-known early statistical systems was IBM's Candide (Berger et al. 1994), which essentially performed machine translation. When you entered French text, it would give you an English translation and vice versa. The model was fed large amounts of data from both French and English so that it could learn translation patterns between both languages and then generate translations based on the likelihood of various translations. Of course, Candide had its limitations. Its performance was dependent heavily on its training data, and because Candide relied on frequency (how often an expression would be used and if it was used at all), it did not do so well for less frequently used expressions.

Today, current LLMs are a more newly evolved form of NLP. While based on statistical principles of modelling language, LLMs implement a level of deep learning and transformer architecture. Deep learning involves envisioning language as a neural network, and transformer architecture involves attention mechanisms that allow the system to weigh the value of different words in a sentence, thereby allowing the LLM to be much more attuned to contextual information and provide more relevant output (Vaswani et al. 2017). What this simply means is that systems like OpenAI's GPT-4 (more commonly accessed through ChatGPT), Anthropic's Claude 3, Google DeepMind's Bard, and Meta AI's LLaMA 3 all seem that much more like a human—which begs the question of whether these systems have finally come close to "understanding" language.

7.2.2 What is natural language understanding?

Natural language understanding (NLU) can be thought of as a kind of NLP work that aims to allow machines to more deeply "understand" language and to "ground it in the world". It has been called "a grand challenge", because we are still nowhere near that sort of understanding (Bender & Koller 2020: 5185). Right now, work in NLU focuses on meaning analysis as well as contextual understanding. For example, it is used in customer service bots to more accurately figure out what the actual intent of the customer is so that the customer can get their concerns addressed more quickly and reliably. They can also be used to more accurately detect the emotions in these chats so as to figure out how frustrated someone might be at having to rebook a flight and plausibly using more targeted strategies to defuse the customer's frustrations, such as to offer vouchers for service not being up to par, among various other things. NLU does have areas of overlap with NLP, such as in sentiment analysis. **Sentiment analysis** identifies the emotional tone of digital texts to figure out if the emotion underlying the message is positive, negative, or neutral and can further weigh these messages in terms of strength of emotion. Sentiment analysis is popularly used as a quick way for businesses trying to understand the large amounts of data that constitute product reviews, social media posts, and survey results, among others. The difference between NLP and NLU's approach, however, shows up in how the latter is meant to go deeper into semantic nuances and may better handle ambiguous or more complex expressions.

All that being said, it should be clear from the Chinese room problem and the octopus test that despite U representing *understanding* in NLU, and despite AI being so advanced these days that their responses astound us, researchers might still be some ways to go from having AI truly understand meaning. NLU, just like NLP, relies on LLMs having large sets of data to train on for the most part. While it is possible for so-called AIs to learn the forms of words or sentences and the contexts in which they appear and predict how they are or should be used, it is not possible to learn actual meaning from these LLMs for the moment, as understanding language at the very basic level is really about synthesising both form and meaning.

7.3 What does sociolinguistics have to do with computing?

At this point, you might begin to ask, what does sociolinguistics have to do with modern-day computing? Why did I say that at the very basic level, one would expect an understanding of language to address issues of form and meaning? While the previous section talked about language as though it was a single entity, as I pointed out, this volume should have provided you with enough insight to realise that language use varies to a large degree. A single language can vary based on where it is spoken and who speaks it (social class, age, gender, community of practice, among others). People can practise the use of more than a single language, too. This means that for a machine to have an extensive understanding of language (just like how you and I understand language), one must also understand how language is used in society (sociolinguistics!).

7.3.1 The challenge of language variation for computing

We can focus first on **variation** within a single language. How well a program or a machine works depends critically on the data that it has been trained on. This should be apparent to those of us who do not speak Standard American English or aspire towards Received Pronunciation.

Siri or whatever GPS system you use in your car may not always understand your "accent". A study from Stanford University found that major automated speech recognition systems misidentified 35 percent of words from users who spoke African American Vernacular English, as compared to 19 percent of words for White speakers (Koenecke et al. 2020). It would come as no surprise if users who speak other varieties of English faced similar issues. Systems that 'speak' may also not be able to respond to you in the same way that you speak. As of 2021, Amazon's Alexa only had one version of a standard American Accent, while Siri from Apple had American, British, Irish, Indian, Australian, and South African accents. While cameo voices include Issa Rae on Google Home and Samuel L. Jackson on Alexa, these African American Vernacular English–speaking voices do not offer true functionality for speakers of this English variety but are rather used for the effect of entertainment (Rangarajan 2021). Similarly, Google Home has an Indian English setting, which speaks Indian-accented English, but which purportedly does not understand Indian-accented English better. And if variation within English is a problem, variation within all the other languages is equally if not more challenging for these "smart" assistants. For example, Google Home's Hindi is actually a highly literary and formal variety of Hindi and not the colloquial version spoken by most Hindi speakers casually (Rangarajan 2021). While it might be challenging to do so, it is useful to consider broadening what goes into a training dataset for these AI systems from a sociolinguistics point of view. For instance, a project in Brazil explored incorporating a database of Brazilian Portuguese vernacular expressions varying by region and situation into an AI (Amadeus, da Silva & Rocha 2024). If AIs are truly to benefit a wider range of users, then we must first begin looking at the ways in which a language can vary sociolinguistically.

7.3.2 The challenge of multilingualism for computing

Just as training datasets should incorporate more diverse data coming from different types of speakers of the same language, there is also increasing recognition that NLP and LLMs should incorporate more diverse languages. **Multilingualism** is an issue for computing. For example, while there are over 65 million speakers of Fula, a West African language, there are extremely few resources available for NLP in the language. Likewise, only a small percentage of the world's languages are represented in important LLMs that exist today (Bommasani et al. 2022). Multilingual models now exist, which build on the latest LLM technologies. These are trained simultaneously on multiple languages and are meant to rise to the challenge of multilingualism. But in actuality, there are some issues with this. There is an assumption that the languages that the machine is simultaneously trained on have shared structures and patterns, and languages with more resources can help train languages with fewer resources (i.e. very little datasets or datasets of questionable quality). However, it is not clear how well these models perform at representing parts of the lower-resource language that may be so drastically different from English (Wu & Dredze 2020). These multilingual models also perform better in languages that are highly similar to the training language set with the most data, and the language of the training set with the most data is almost always English. These are but some issues that have to be resolved before we get to asking if the model can accurately translate from one language to another (particularly if one of these languages has much fewer resources) or if a model can handle codeswitching data, among other sorts of natural multilingual phenomena.

7.3.3 Human-computer interaction and sociolinguistics

Apart from issues of sociolinguistics that can arise when developing any new technology that uses language, we can also look at how new technology results in novel ways of **interaction between human and computers**. Research shows that human beings do interact with computer systems as though they are real social agents, just like how Weizenbaum's secretary started forming an attachment to ELIZA (see Section 2). Humans are shown to apply similar sorts of social rules and expectations to computers, even to the extent of applying gender stereotypes to computers and ethnically identifying with computers (Nass & Moon 2000): Participants in an experiment with tutor computers presenting topics on "computers and technology" and "love and relationships" found the female-voiced computer more informative about love and relationships as compared to the male-voiced computer, whereas the male-voiced computer was perceived as being more informative about computers than the female-voiced computer. In a different experiment, participants were presented hypothetical dilemmas where two courses of action could ensue, and they had to ask a Korean or Caucasian video-faced computer agent what decision it would make. Predictably, participants faced with a computer agent of the "same" ethnicity perceived the agent to be more attractive, trustworthy, persuasive, and intelligent and more likely to make similar decisions as themselves, compared to when they faced a computer agent of different ethnicity. Humans do all of these things, even though they recognise that computers are not human (Nass, Steuer & Tauber 1994). Apparently, human beings are polite to computers, even if they know they are computers! With the prevalence of computers, as well as huge advancements in AI and the development of intelligent chatbots, we see more possibility of computers becoming significant actors in society whose actions are evaluated as meaningful and intentional (Lang et al. 2013), which raises the question of whether computers can be sociolinguistic actors too. For instance, computers might possibly be seen to evoke a certain **sociolinguistic style** or persona type or even engage in **politeness theory** (humans are said to have positive face needs, which mean they want to be valued and appreciated, and negative face needs, which focus on their desire to feel like they have a freedom of choice and to not feel imposed upon; more later). The opportunities of viewing these new technological advancements through the lens of sociolinguistics are limitless.

7.4 Sociolinguistics in online communication

In fact, technology is not something that sociolinguists are just about now paying attention to. Sociolinguistics has been studied in online communications, which include communications on a wide range of platforms, including text messaging when text messaging was more popularly used, media platforms like YouTube, and social networking sites such as Facebook and Twitter (now X). Virtually any topic in sociolinguistics can also be studied in online communications.

7.4.1 Lexical and grammatical innovations online and offline

A major locus of research in sociolinguistics is language change (see especially Chapter 2 on variation in sociolinguistics), which can involve **lexical innovations** and **lexical changes** or **changes in the patterns of grammar**. In China, Shitizen Chinglish, also known as Net Chinglish or New Chinglish, arose from deliberate and subversive creation of new forms of English that are meant to express, in addition to other meanings, its creator's "social dissatisfaction" (Wei 2018: 15). Interesting new words that have emerged include *shitizen*, which plays on the phonological distinction between S and SH, which some speakers of Chinese find hard; *stuck market* instead of stock market; and *niubility* or *newbility*, which indicates the ability to boast, formidability, incredibility, or awesomeness, arising from the Chinese term *niubi* 牛逼, which was originally a taboo term used to refer to a cow's genitals that later on gained popular usage as a verb meaning 'to boast'. This variety of Chinglish has taken off because the state monitors keep a closer watch on Chinese than English, and netizens are better able to express what they deem more subversive in this variety of Chinglish. In a separate study on Chinese itself, it is observed that Chinese internet language itself is now used outside of online communications (Gao 2011), including foreign loanwords such as *zaixian* 在线 'at line', to mean online, and *ku* 酷 'cruel' to express the concept of cool. Grammatical change has also taken place, for example, in the use of nouns as adjectives, where *cai* 菜 'vegetable' is used to mean that someone or something is weak and incapable, and *yangguang* 阳光 'sunlight' is used as an adjective to describe someone or something as being "healthy and optimistic". Elsewhere in the world, similar types of phenomena are taking place. In Bosnia, *vlog* (clipping and blending of 'video' and 'blog') has not only been incorporated in Bosnian; the word has now adopted Bosnian linguistic features, so the form *vlogovanja* 'of vlogging' exists, where *-ovanja* indicates the genitive case singular to mean 'of doing something' and *vlogovanje* 'vlogging' indicates a verbal noun formed from a Bosnian verb form, *vlogovati* 'to vlog', rather than the original English noun *vlog* (Tankosić & Dovchin 2023). New words or forms are not always invented, by the way. In English, in addition to new words from technology, the prevalence of social media and online communication has brought about **semantic broadening** as well, where terms such as "wall", "like", and "status" receive additional meanings beyond their original lexical meanings, and these are now used in daily offline communication as well (West & Trester 2013).

> **Online speak in your online communities**
>
> What are the online communities that you belong to? Do these communities have words or phrases that are uniquely invented for the use of that community? Or do they have words and phrases that are used differently in that community as compared to how they are used offline?

These new ways of using language online can also be dealt with through the lens of different sociolinguistics subfields.

7.4.2 Language ideologies, translanguaging, and more

One can also observe **language ideologies** (recall Chapter 3) at play in new media. For example, a study of text messaging in the town of Malindi, Kenya, shows that young people are using rapid codeswitching and a form of condensed, abbreviated English in their messages to index a "modern, mobile, self-fashioning, sexy, and irreverent persona", while their use of Kigiriama indexes local values and "reroots them in the gravitas of social obligations and respect relationships" (Mcintosh 2010: 337). It is also interesting to explore how the online space allows for an expression of personal linguistic ideologies. For example, a Mongolian undergraduate studying English may choose to use the Cyrillic Mongolian script on Facebook rather than a Mongolian Roman script, which is what many other Mongolian Facebook users are doing, as a way of expressing pride in their own writing system and out of fear that Cyrillic scripts may one day go the way of the old Mongolian script, which was previously replaced during a socialist era (Dovchin 2019). One can also go to the extent of talking about how online varieties such as Shitizen Chinglish have created a new space for **translanguaging**, where new identities and ideologies can come into play (Wei 2016) when these online varieties become additional resources in a speakers' toolkit of language(s) (see Chapter 3 on multilingualism)—think about how a user of Shitizen Chinglish might be able to express sentiments that they are not able to express in Chinese and still not run afoul of state monitors. In yet another approach that utilises politeness theory, we can even look at how users of different social media platforms such as Facebook utilise strategies to stay polite by taking into consideration the face needs of their interlocutors while communicating online (West & Trester 2013). Again, there are multiple methods and approaches in sociolinguistics through which we can make sense of online communications.

> ## Politeness theory on social platforms
>
> **Threatening one's positive face** would mean expressing something that possibly infringes upon a person's need to feel valued and appreciated, and **threatening one's negative face** would infringe upon one's need to feel a freedom of action and not to be imposed upon (see end of Section 3 of this chapter). When sending messages over social media, what strategies do you use to avoid threatening someone's positive face, and what are the strategies that you use for mitigating threat to one's negative face? For example, I could put a smiley face ☺ at the end of my comments to an Instagram post to come across as more positively polite. Do you use different strategies for when the post is set to "public" versus when you are sending direct messages, and why? Reflect on your own strategies.

7.4.3 Online speak as a reflection of offline speak

Notably, apart from studying the sociolinguistics of online language use itself, online communications can be sometimes used as a way of studying wider patterns in the varieties of the language. A corpus study of Hong Kong Twitter (now X) was used to examine patterns in the Hong Kong English used in tweets, such as whether clauses that use the copula are preferred over not using the copula ("his hands *are* too full"—following English rules—versus "his hands too full"— following Chinese rules) and, similarly, whether adverbs are preferred preverbally versus clause-finally ("I *already* went there" versus "I went there *already*"). Results show that the distribution patterns found generally aligned with known descriptions of oral and written mainstream Hong Kong English (Gonzales 2023). In a separate corpus study of

Colloquial Singapore English that collected data in the form of Whats App messages, researchers were able to study how a sentence final particle, *sia*, developed new social meanings as an index of coolness, in addition to an original vulgar connotation that is only understood by speakers of Malay, from which the word originally was derived (Hafiz et al. 2023). A separate study looking at social media texts (including WhatsApp messages, Instagram posts, Reddit posts, Facebook statuses, and responses to newspaper articles online) collected from Bruneians and Malaysians shows that their multilingual repertoires extend beyond Malay and English, considering that both communities of speakers are highly multilingual (McLellan 2022). Studies such as these show us that online communications can sometimes be an effective and useful lens on changes in language use that are taking place more widely in society.

7.5 Computational tools for sociolinguistics

Sociolinguistics is a useful tool for studying phenomena brought on by these new waves and advances in technology, just as computational tools can also be used meaningfully for the study of sociolinguistics. Some of the computational tools that are commonly used by sociolinguists include speech analysis software; transcription software and forced aligners; survey tools; statistical tools; and text, multimedia, and corpus analysis tools.

7.5.1 Software for speech analysis and synthesis

One of the most commonly used computational tools in sociolinguistics is **Praat**, open-source **software designed for the analysis and synthesis of speech** (Boersma & Weenink 2013). It is useful for various things, such as generating spectrograms (see Figure 7.1) and providing insight on the acoustic properties of speech sounds, including how loud they are, how long they are held for, and what frequencies they are at, among other sorts of information one might be interested in.

Praat is therefore used by sociolinguists interested in the qualities of sound, be it in identification of the qualities of sounds that are associated with round shapes versus spikey shapes (*bouba* vs. *kiki*) (D'Onofrio 2014); in the study of sounds that may change or stay stable over time, such as -ING in varieties such as Australian English, -ING being a linguistic variant which is said to be relatively stable (Travis,

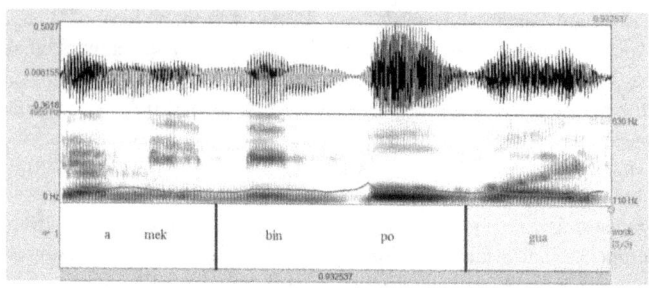

Figure 7.1 Example of spectrogram generated in Praat (*amék binpo gua* 'take my handkerchief' in Baba Malay) (Lee 2022)

Grama & Purser 2023); or even in how particular voice qualities might index particular styles and affect, such as how creaky voice (or a raspy, scratchy voice quality also known as 'vocal fry') and a slower speech rate (in addition to stillness in body posture) are used by cisgender young men who self-identified as being chill or low energy in a Bay Area public arts high school (Pratt 2023). Praat can also be used to synthesise sounds for experiments. In one experiment, a vowel that indexed refinedness in Baba Malay was raised in Praat to various degrees and presented to listeners who had to rate if a more raised vowel came across as being more refined than a less raised vowel (Lee 2020) (raising usually means that the vowel is produced with a higher tongue body closer to the roof of the mouth) (see Section 7.3). For the majority of sociolinguists who work on sound, Praat is perhaps one of the best-known, longest-surviving, and still relevant computational tools.

7.5.2 Transcription software

Yet another type of computational tool is the **transcription software** that sociolinguists use. It may not be apparent how difficult the task of transcription is until you have had the opportunity to try it for yourself. You might be transcribing a recording that is of poor fidelity, dealing with background noise, overlapping speech, and a language variety that you are less familiar with. With that, computerised transcription software makes the transcription task that much easier by allowing you to play back easily, control playback speed, insert time stamps or align the transcription directly with speech stream, and handle overlapping speech where this might be an issue. In addition to Praat, commonly used transcription tools include the EUDICO Linguistic Annotator (also known as ELAN) (The Language Archive 2024) as well as Transcriber AG (Paci et al. 2011). Transcription software forms the basic toolkit of sociolinguists, alongside Praat, given that most sociolinguists work on speech production data. Of course, you can transcribe using a separate media player and a word processor, but using transcription software makes things a whole lot more efficient, so why not? Today, with the rise of automation, automatic transcription software has become more popular, but it still requires a bit of finessing on the part of the sociolinguists, given that most was developed for business usage and may be less suited for capturing varieties of English apart from Standard English or other languages apart from English.

7.5.3 Forced aligners

Alongside transcription software is the **forced aligner**. The forced aligner is a computational tool that aligns transcription more accurately onto the speech stream. This can be done to a high level of detail, such as to the level of individual sounds, which is what sociolinguists studying speech sounds need. The forced aligner is able to do so because it has been trained on the properties of speech sounds and the transcriptions these sounds are most likely to map onto. An algorithm is usually also applied to ensure that each audio signal is mapped onto a transcription. The most commonly used forced aligners today include Penn Forced Aligner (Yuan & Liberman 2008) and FAVE (Forced Alignment and Vowel Extraction) (Rosenfelder et al. 2022). They allow sociolinguists to do things such as align transcription with speech at a detailed level and quickly pick out the consonants, vowels, or other speech features they want to look at—while plausibly not the most exciting sounding computational tool, the role of the forced aligner cannot be disregarded. However, like automatic transcribers, forced aligners are mostly developed for English and other dominant languages. A lot more can be done for less-represented languages.

7.5.4 Computational survey tools

Another important computational tool in the sociolinguists' toolkit is the **survey tool.** These can range from Google Forms to Amazon Mechanical Turk (2005) to more comprehensive online survey and research platforms such as Qualtrics (2005a). Each has its own quirks and pros and cons. Google Forms (2008) might be simpler to set up and have lower technological barriers to entry. MTurk (2005) allows you to post surveys that quickly get picked up by a diverse group of "workers" around the world that you have technically crowdsourced the task to and who are happy to do these surveys because they are compensated financially for doing so. Qualtrics is more expensive, but it is highly comprehensive, allowing you to do various types of surveys with multiple types of answer options (from ratings to multiple choices, text entry, etc.), with the added ability to customise the survey taker's experience based on their responses. All of these modern computational survey tools allow survey takers to respond at a time that is convenient for them and can potentially be used to collect data much more quickly from many more people than a traditional pen and paper survey would allow for. The modern computational survey tool also provides for easier statistical analysis since the data does not have to be transferred from paper to computer, and some programs even offer instantaneous statistical analysis. These tools can be used for any survey that does not have to be conducted face to face or that does not require speech production. For example, MTurk has been used for acceptability judgement tasks, where respondents say if some expression is acceptable in their language (Sprouse 2011), and Qualtrics has been used to run matched guise tasks to uncover attitudes towards particular speakers and their stereotypes (Ruthan 2024).

7.5.5 Other computational tools for quantitative and qualitative analysis

Finally, computational tools are used for **statistical analysis**, as well as **text, multimedia, and corpora analysis.** These are particularly useful when sorting and analysing massive amounts of data, be it quantitative or qualitative. Programs such as R (R Development Core Team 2021) and SPSS (2023a) are used for large amounts of quantitative work that undergirds variationist sociolinguistics. Other programs are useful for dealing with qualitative data from sociolinguistic interviews, various sorts of discourse, and even videos. Programs such as nVivo (2023b) are used for classifying data, annotating it for further analysis, and in the actual analysis itself. Likewise, there is a whole slew of concordance tools such as AntConc (Anthony 2024) to make sense of the corpuses that sociolinguists may use in their work to compare keywords and observe where they occur. AntConc is particularly useful for large datasets, and corpus developers usually tailor their corpuses with AntConc in mind (Gonzales 2023).

While computational tools come and go, the ones mentioned here have been the mainstays of sociolinguists for a while and are but some examples of the computational tools that they use—showing that computational tools are useful for the study of sociolinguistics, just as perspectives from sociolinguistics should be incorporated for the successful implementation of technology.

7.6 A final word

Having delved into what is perhaps one of the most current topics in sociolinguistics, we have come to the end of our whirlwind tour. This chapter is plausibly an appropriate chapter to end the volume on, because it demonstrates how the study of sociolinguistics is constantly evolving, just as society is constantly changing. A fuller understanding of the human language capacity necessarily entails how we interact with that ever-changing world. That being said, this volume is by no means exhaustive, and it does not aim to be so given its exploratory nature. What I hope, however, is that this book has done enough to pique your curiosity in sociolinguistics and that you are now equipped and motivated to take it further.

References

Aamoth, Doug. 2014. Interview with Eugene Goostman, the fake kid who passed the turing test. *TIME*. https://time.com/2847900/eugene-goostman-turing-test/. (6 August, 2024).

Amadeus, Marcellus, José Roberto Homeli da Silva & João Victor Pessoa Rocha. 2024. Bridging the language gap: Integrating language variations into conversational AI agents for enhanced user engagement. *Proceedings of the 1st Workshop towards Ethical and Inclusive Conversational AI: Language Attitudes, Linguistic Diversity, and Language Rights (TEICAI 2024)*, 16–20. Association for Computational Linguistics.

Amazon Mechanical Turk. 2005. Seattle, Washington: Amazon.

Anthony, Laurence. 2024. AntConc (Version 4.3.1). Tokyo, Japan: Waseda University.

Bender, Emily M. & Alexander Koller. 2020. Climbing towards NLU: On meaning, form, and understanding in the age of data. In Dan Jurafsky, Joyce Chai, Natalie Schluter & Joel Tetreault (eds.), *Proceedings of the 58th Annual Meeting of the Association for Computational Linguistics*, 5185–5198. Online: Association for Computational Linguistics. https://doi.org/10.18653/v1/2020.acl-main.463.

Berger, Adam L., Peter F. Brown, Stephen A. Della Pietra, Vincent J. Della Pietra, John R. Gillett, John D. Lafferty, Robert L. Mercer, Harry Printz & Luboš Ureš. 1994. The Candide system for machine translation. In *Proceedings of the Workshop on Human Language Technology—HLT '94*, 157. Plainsboro, NJ: Association for Computational Linguistics. https://doi.org/10.3115/1075812.1075844.

Boersma, Paul & David Weenink. 2013. Praat: Doing Phonetics by Computer [Computer Program]. Version 5.3.59. www.praat.org/ (20 November, 2013).

Bommasani, Rishi, Drew A. Hudson, Ehsan Adeli, Russ Altman, Simran Arora, Sydney von Arx, Michael S. Bernstein, et al. 2022. On the Opportunities and Risks of Foundation Models. Centre for Research on Foundation Models, Stanford University: arXiv. http://arxiv.org/abs/2108.07258. (14 August, 2024).

D'Onofrio, Annette. 2014. Phonetic detail and dimensionality in sound-shape correspondences: Refining the Bouba-Kiki paradigm. *Language and Speech*. SAGE Publications Ltd 57(3). 367–393. https://doi.org/10.1177/0023830913507694.

Dovchin, Sender. 2019. *Language, Social Media and Ideologies: Translingual Englishes, Facebook and Authenticities*. Springer International Publishing.

Gao, Liwei. 2011. Synchronic variation or diachronic change: A sociolinguistic study of Chinese internet language. In *Chinese Under Globalization*, 7–28. World Scientific. https://doi.org/10.1142/9789814350709_0002.

Gonzales, Wilkinson Daniel Wong. 2023. From tweets to trends: Analyzing sociolinguistic variation and change using the Twitter Corpus of English in Hong Kong (TCOEHK). *Asian Englishes*. https://doi.org/10.1080/13488678.2023.2251771.

Google Forms. 2008. Mountain View, California: Google.

Hafiz, Mohamed, Mie Hiramoto, Jakob R. E. Leimgruber, Wilkinson Daniel Wong Gonzales & Jun Jie Lim. 2023. Sociolinguistic variation in Colloquial Singapore English sia. *World Englishes* n/a(n/a). https://doi.org/10.1111/weng.12700.

IBM SPSS Statistics for Windows. 2023a. Version 29.0.2.0. Armonk, New York: IBM Corp.

Koenecke, Allison, Andrew Nam, Emily Lake, Joe Nudell, Minnie Quartey, Zion Mengesha, Connor Toups, John R. Rickford, Dan Jurafsky & Sharad Goel. 2020. Racial disparities in automated speech recognition. *Proceedings of the National Academy of Sciences*. Proceedings of the National Academy of Sciences 117(14). 7684–7689. https://doi.org/10.1073/pnas.1915768117.

Lang, Helmut, Melina Klepsch, Florian Nothdurft, Tina Seufert & Wolfgang Minker. 2013. Are computers still social actors? In *Human Factors in Computing Systems*, 859–864. https://doi.org/10.1145/2468356.2468510.

The Language Archive. 2024. ELAN (Version 6.8). Nijmegen: Max Planck Institute for Psycholinguistics. https://archive.mpi.nl/tla/elan.

Lee, Nala H. 2020. Style variation in the second formant: What does it mean to be "refined" in Baba Malay? *Language Ecology*. John Benjamins 4(1). 115–130. https://doi.org/10.1075/le.00012.lee.

Lee, Nala H. 2022. *A Grammar of Modern Baba Malay*. De Gruyter Mouton.

Mcintosh, Janet. 2010. Mobile phones and Mipoho's prophecy: The powers and dangers of flying language. *American Ethnologist* 37(2). 337–353. https://doi.org/10.1111/j.1548-1425.2010.01259.x.

McLellan, James. 2022. Malay and English language contact in social media texts in Brunei Darussalam and Malaysia. *Frontiers in Communication* 7. https://doi.org/10.3389/fcomm.2022.810838.

Nass, Clifford & Youngme Moon. 2000. Machines and mindlessness: Social responses to computers. *Journal of Social Issues* 56(1). 81–103. https://doi.org/10.1111/0022-4537.00153.

Nass, Clifford, Jonathan Steuer & Ellen R. Tauber. 1994. Computers are social actors. In *Human Factors in Computing Systems*, 72–78. Boston.

nVivo 14. 2023b. Denver, Colorado: Lumivero.

Oremus, Will. 2024. AI researchers call for "personhood credentials" as bots grow smarter—The Washington Post. Washington, DC. www.washingtonpost.com/politics/2024/08/21/human-bot-personhood-credentials-worldcoin/. (22 August, 2024).

Paci, Giulio, Elie Roux, Edouard Geoffrois & Karim Boudahmane. 2011. Transcriber AG. DGA. https://transag.sourceforge.net.

Pratt, Teresa. 2023. Affect in sociolinguistic style. *Language in Society* 52(1). 1–26. https://doi.org/10.1017/S0047404521000774.

Qualtrics. 2005a. Provo, Utah: Qualtrics. www.qualtrics.com.

Rangarajan, Sinduja. 2021. Hey Siri—why don't you understand more people who talk like me? *Mother Jones*. www.motherjones.com/media/2021/02/digital-assistants-accents-english-race-google-siri-alexa/. (14 August, 2024).

R Development Core Team. 2021. R: A language and environment for statistical computing. Vienna: R Foundation for Statistical Computing. www.R-project.org.

Rosenfelder, Ingrid, Josef Fruehwald, Christian Brickhouse, Keelan Evanini, Scott Seyfarth, Kyle Gorman, Hilary Prichard, & Jiahong Yuan. 2022. FAVE (Forced Alignment and Vowel Extraction) Program Suite v2.0.0/*zenodo*.

Ruthan, Mohammed Q. 2024. Salient sociophonetic features, stereotypes, and attitudes toward Jazani Arabic. *Humanities and Social Sciences Communications*. Palgrave 11(1). 1–12. https://doi.org/10.1057/s41599-024-02832-w.

Searle, John R. 1980. Minds, brains, and programs. *Behavioral and Brain Sciences* 3(3). 417–424. https://doi.org/10.1017/S0140525X00005756.

Sprouse, Jon. 2011. A validation of Amazon Mechanical Turk for the collection of acceptability judgments in linguistic theory. *Behavior Research Methods* 43(1). 155–167. https://doi.org/10.3758/s13428-010-0039-7.

Tankosić, Ana & Sender Dovchin. 2023. The impact of social media in the sociolinguistic practices of the peripheral post-socialist contexts. *International Journal of Multilingualism*. Routledge 20(3). 869–890. https://doi.org/10.1080/14790718.2021.1917582.

Travis, Catherine E., James Grama & Benjamin Purser. 2023. Stability and change in (Ing): Ethnic and grammatical variation over time in Australian English. *English World-Wide*. John Benjamins 44(3). 435–469. https://doi.org/10.1075/eww.22043.tra.

Turing, Alan M. 1950. Computing machinery and intelligence. *Mind* 59. 433–460. https://doi.org/10.1093/mind/LIX.236.433.

Vaswani, Ashish, Noam Shazeer, Niki Parmar, Jakob Uszkoreit, Llion Jones, Aidan N. Gomez, Łukasz Kaiser & Illia Polosukhin. 2017. Attention is all you need. *Advances in Neural Information Processing Systems*, vol. 30, Curran Associates, Inc. https://proceedings.neurips.cc/paper_files/paper/2017/hash/3f5ee243547dee91fbd053c1c4a845aa-Abstract.html. (7 August, 2024).

Wei, Li. 2016. New Chinglish and the post-multilingualism challenge: Translanguaging ELF in China. *Journal of English as a Lingua Franca* 5(1). www.degruyter.com/document/doi/10.1515/jelf-2016-0001/html?lang=en.

Wei, Li. 2018. Translanguaging as a practical theory of language. *Applied Linguistics* 39(1). 9–30. https://doi.org/10.1093/applin/amx039.

Weizenbaum, Joseph. 1976. *Computer Power and Human Reason: From Judgement to Calculation*. CA: W.H. Freeman and Company.

West, Laura & Anna Marie Trester. 2013. Facework on Facebook: Conversations on social media. In Deborah Tannen & Anna Marie Trester (eds.), *Discourse 2.0: Language and New Media*, 133–154. Georgetown University Press.

Wu, Shijie & Mark Dredze. 2020. Are all languages created equal in multilingual BERT? In Spandana Gella, Johannes Welbl, Marek Rei, Fabio Petroni, Patrick Lewis, Emma Strubell, Minjoon Seo & Hannaneh Hajishirzi (eds.), *Proceedings of the 5th Workshop on Representation Learning for NLP*, 120–130. Online: Association for Computational Linguistics. https://doi.org/10.18653/v1/2020.repl4nlp-1.16.

Yuan, Jiahong & Mark Liberman. 2008. Speaker identification on the SCOTUS corpus. *Journal of the Acoustical Society of America* 123(5). 3878.

Short glossary of terms relating to other branches of linguistics

Affixation: Affixes are added either to the beginning, end, or even middle of the word to modify its meaning or its part of speech. Examples of affixes are *un-* and *-ing* in the word *undoing*.

Approximant /r/ : This sort of 'r' sound is made where the tongue comes close to the roof of the mouth but does not make full contact with it or vibrate against it.

Aspect: Aspect deals with how an event unfolds, such as whether an event is completed or is still ongoing.

Aspiration: Aspiration is the obvious puff of air that one produces when saying consonants such as /p/, /t/, and /k/.

Classifier: A word or morpheme that is used with a noun to indicate the category or type of object the noun refers to, such as its shape, size, or function.

Copula: A word that links a noun subject to its complement, which is usually a word or descriptive term that identifies the noun. An example of a copula is the word *is* in the sentence, *The moon is round*.

Creaky voice: Also known as 'vocal fry', creaky voice refers to a raspy, scratchy voice quality that is created by compressing the vocal folds very tightly and minimising airflow passing through them.

Determiner: A word or morpheme that is used alongside a noun to make it more specific, such as its definiteness or its number, among other sorts of information.

Diphthong: A diphthong is a sequence of two vowel sounds within the same syllable—they start with one sound and end on another. An example of a diphthong is the /aʊ/ sound in words such *house* and *cloud*.

Glide: Glides are consonants that involve a quick, smooth movement from one position in the mouth to another. An example of a glide is the /w/ sound in words like *wet*.

Labial: Labial sounds are produced using lips. An example of a labial sound is the /m/ sound in *monkey*.

Modality: Modality deals with people's attitudes to things, such as if they are obligated to do something or if one can make a strong guess about something in the world. For example, *John has to be there* can reflect both of these stances.

Morpheme: A morpheme is the smallest meaningful unit in a language. It can either be a word or a part making up a word, such as *un-* and *do* in *undo*.

Noun phrase: a noun phrase is a group of words that includes a noun (usually a concrete or abstract thing) and additional information about it.

Plosives: A plosive is a speech sound that is made by creating a complete obstruction in the mouth and then releasing it suddenly. Examples of plosives in English include /d/ and /t/ in English.

Prefix: Prefixes are attached to the beginning of a word to modify its meaning or part of speech.

Retroflex: A retroflex is produced by curling the tip of the tongue towards the roof of the mouth.

Rhoticity: Rhoticity refers to the pronunciation of /r/, whereas dropping one's /r/ is non-rhotic.

Tapped /r/: The tapped /r/ refers to 'r' which is produced when the tongue taps the roof of the mouth in the alveolar region quickly.

Trilled /r/: The trilled /r/ is produced when the tongue vibrates against the roof of the mouth quickly.

Velar: Velar sounds are made when the back of the tongue comes close to or touches the velum, which is the soft part found towards the back of the roof of the mouth. An example of a velar is /g/ in 'give'.

Voiced: Voiced speech sounds are produced with vibrating vocal cords as air passes through them.

Voiceless: Voiceless speech sounds are produced without vibration in the vocal cords as air passes through them.

Index

Académie Française 53
accent 4–5, 14, 36, 125, 128, 134, 157
acceptability judgement task 27, 166
accommodation theory 42
acoustic 30, 163
acrolectal 89
additive bilingualism 57, 59–60
adolescents 27, 28
adstrate language 82
affixation 26–27, 172
African American Vernacular English 14, 36, 86, 125–126, 137, 141, 147
age 5–6, 25–26, 36–37, 77, 104, 108, 116–117
age-grading 37
Ainu 102
Akuntsú 103
Alaska 74
American Indian 103
apparent time 36
approximant /r/ 25, 37
Arawak-Taíno 75
Argentina 12
artificial intelligence (AI) 16, 148–159
Aruba 90
Aruban Papiamento 90

Aslian 56
aspect 79
aspiration 1, 25, 172
Assyrian 7, 48
Atayal 82
audience design 42–43
Australia 10, 33, 77, 112–113, 128–129, 131, 157, 163
Australian English 163
Austronesian 56, 116
authenticity 23, 36, 90, 115
authorship attribution 132–133
awakening languages 109

Baba Malay 1, 39, 56, 82–83, 85, 87, 90, 112, 116–117, 164
Babylonian 7, 48
Bahasa Indonesia 52–53
balanced bilingualism 59
Bantu languages 75, 77
basilectal 89
Beijing Mandarin 6, 32
Belfast 37
Belgium 48
bilingualism 7, 10, 47–67
biocultural diversity 100–101
Black 86, 125–127, 137
Black Tai 113–114
Bolivia 98
Bosnian 160

Brazil 98, 103, 157
Brazilian Portuguese 157
Breath of Life workshops 113
British Columbia 74
British Isles 33
Brunei 163
Burmese 29, 66–67

California 4, 41, 74, 125, 139
Cameroonian Pidgin 89
Canada 48, 57, 77, 123–124, 136
Candide 154
Cantonese 4, 9–10, 34, 54, 73, 80
Cape Town 90
Caribbean 85–86, 137
Catalan 128
Catalonia 128
Caucasian language 103
censorship 129
Chabacano 56, 90
chatbots 16, 149, 159
ChatGPT 148–151, 155
Chile 11
Chinese 4, 8–9, 26, 54, 56, 65, 82, 85–86, 88, 102, 112, 160–161
Chinese Pidgin English 9, 88
Chinese room problem 150, 152–153, 156
Chinglish 160–161
Chinook Wawa 74
Circassian genocide 103
cisgender 164
classifier 32, 90, 172
coarseness 116–117
Cockney English 4
codemixing 63–64
codeswitching 8–9, 63–65, 87, 90, 158, 161
Collins COBUILD 29

Colloquial Singapore English 2, 49, 163
colonisation 52, 75, 79, 87, 103
Colossus 149
community of practice 34, 39–40, 156
community work 117, 128
computational tools 163–167
computing 15–16, 148–167
consonant 29–30, 36, 165
contact languages 9–11, 30, 56, 72–90
copula 98, 162, 172
corpus 15, 27–29, 87, 89, 162–163, 167
Corpus of Contemporary American English (COCA) 28–29
Corpus of Singapore English Messages (CoSEM) 15, 29
corpus planning 54–55
courts 14, 49, 126, 131, 136–138, 141
covert prestige 32, 88
creaky voice 164, 172
Cree 77
creole 9–11, 50, 56, 72–90, 99, 102–103, 142
creole continuum 89
Croatia 130
Cushitic languages 77

deadnaming 130
defamation 131
deletion 39
Detroit 127
dialect 3–5, 33, 39, 102, 135
diglossia 9, 49–50, 89
diphthong 22, 116, 172
domains of language use 8, 51, 53, 88
dormant language 97, 106, 109, 113

Eastern-European 128, 131
education 25, 31, 50, 54–60, 65, 82, 84, 87–88, 102, 104–105, 112, 123–124, 128
elite bilingualism 60
ELIZA 153
English 1–2, 4, 6–10, 14, 16, 22, 25–26, 29–31, 33–34, 37, 39, 42, 48–49, 52–57, 63–67, 73–80, 83, 85–89, 101, 125, 127–128, 136–137, 139, 141–143, 154, 157–158, 160–163, 165
Eskimo Trade Jargon 74
ethics 38
ethnicity 35, 85, 99, 159
ethnography 34, 40, 114–115, 128
Etruscan 11
executive control 7, 61
Expanded Graded Intergenerational Disruption Scale (EGIDS) 105–106
extinct languages 109

female 26, 28, 33–34, 36, 126, 129, 158
Finland 113
Fongbe 81
forced alignment 165
forensic linguistics 14, 132–134, 138–139
formality 6, 23, 32, 40–42, 49–50, 85, 90, 115, 157
founder principle 79–80
France 116
Francoprovençal 116
French 30–31, 39, 50, 53–54, 57, 65, 74–75, 77, 85, 87–88, 102–103, 116, 124, 136, 154
fricative 36
friend of a friend 37–38
Fula 157

gender 6, 16, 23, 27, 33–36, 126, 130, 158, 164
generative AI 148
German 54, 125
Gilbertese 102
glide 39, 172
Graded Intergenerational Disruption Scale (GIDS) 104–105
Guadaloupe 85
Guadalupian Kréyòl 86
Guangzhou 73
Gulf Coast 73
Gurindji Kriol 10, 39, 77

Haiti 75
Haitian Creole 50, 75, 81, 90
Hakka 4, 54
Hawai'i 10, 13–14, 33, 36, 57, 76, 78–81, 85–86, 99, 112
Hawai'i Creole English 10, 33, 76, 79–81, 85–86
Hebrew 49
high school 30, 34, 39, 41, 164
Hindi 50, 157
Hiri Motu 73–74
Hmong-Mien languages 99
Hokkaido 102
Hokkien 4, 26, 82–83, 142–143
Hong Kong 34, 162
Hull 28
human-computer interaction 16, 153, 158
hypercorrection 41–42

Idaho 74
identity 10, 12, 25, 32, 35, 77, 87–88, 99, 106, 116
immersion language programme 57, 60, 112–113
India 7, 50
Indian 25, 35–37, 54, 56

indigenous languages 56, 89, 101, 112–113, 124
Indonesia 52, 82, 98
Indus script 99
ING variant 33–34
Inner Mongolia 102
insertion 64
intelligence 61, 148
intergenerational transmission 104–105, 107–108, 111–112, 114, 124
isiXhosa 128
Islamophobia 130

Jamaica 85
Jamaican Creole 85–87, 89, 90, 141–142
Japan 3–4, 10, 53, 102, 129
Japanese 3–4, 29, 66, 82
jargon 73–74
Javanese 6, 16, 41
jurilinguistics 136
justice 13–14, 60, 122–143

Kallawaya 98
Kenya 161
Kigiriama 161
Kiribati 102
Korean 34
Kreol Morisien 84
Kriol 77
Kuki-Chin 128
Kurdish 102

labial 39, 173
language acquisition 8, 27, 58, 78
language attitudes 12, 27, 30–31, 36, 52, 60–62, 88, 90, 101–102, 109, 166
language bioprogram hypothesis 10, 78–79

language classes 112
language crimes 13–14, 129–137
language death 12, 97
language diversity 98
language documentation 12, 38, 109–111, 115
language endangerment 11, 13, 51, 87, 97–117, 122, 124
Language Endangerment Index (LEI) 108
language ideologies 51–56, 60, 101–102, 161
language loss 11–13, 97–103, 117
language nests 112
language obsolescence 11, 116
language policy 8, 51, 53–57, 82, 87, 102, 107, 109, 149
language purity 52
language revitalisation 13, 57, 109, 111–114, 128
language shift 11, 13, 77, 89, 101–104, 111, 114
language status 4, 12, 25, 33, 55, 59–60, 87, 106–107, 122
language variation 32, 114, 117, 156
language vitality 89, 100, 104, 106–108
Lánnang-uè 26
large language models (LLMs) 148, 155–158
last speaker 12, 97, 109
legalese 135
Lesoto 128
lexical change 160
lexical innovation 160
lexicon 4, 77, 81, 83
lexifier language 78, 84
Light Walpiri 77
lingua franca 56, 73, 83–84
linguistic descriptivism 55

linguistic discrimination 12, 14, 86, 103, 122, 125–127, 137
linguistic genocide 103
linguistic hegemony 52
linguistic insecurity 102–103, 117
linguistic prescriptivism 54
linguistic rights 122–124
linguistic variable 24, 25, 32, 43
loanwords 65–67, 160
London 149
Louisiana 75, 103, 136–137
Louisiana Creole 75, 103
Luxembourg 54

Ma'a 77
machine translation 15, 29, 153–154
Malacca Creole Portuguese 56, 85
Malay 8, 29, 41, 54, 55–56, 82–83, 143, 163
Malaysia 8, 30, 39, 55–56, 82, 163
Malaysian English 25, 35
male 5–6, 26, 28, 33–36, 49, 126, 158
Mandarin 4, 32, 39, 54, 56, 62, 84, 102, 143
Māori 57, 112
market language ideology 53
maroonage 75
marriage 35, 72, 82–83, 85, 88
Martha's Vineyard 22–23, 116
master-apprentice programmes 112–113
matched guise task 30–31, 90, 117, 166
Mauritius 84
Mediterranean 7, 48, 84
mesolectal 89
metalinguistic awareness 62
Michif 77, 87–88

Milton Keynes 28
minoritisation 13
minority language 26, 50, 52, 57, 59–60, 114
Miranda rights 138–139
mixed language 9–10, 72–73, 77, 81, 83
Mobilian Jargon 73–74
modality 79, 173
Mon 66–67
Mongolian 161
monolingualism 7, 48, 51–52, 60, 65
Montana 74
Montreal 30–31
morpheme 34, 115, 173
morphology 26
mother tongue 53–54, 56
Motu 73–74
multilingualism 7–9, 11, 47–67, 72, 97, 157–158
music 86
mutiny 75
mutual intelligibility 4

nation 7, 48, 51–55
Native American 73, 103
Natural Language Processing (NLP) 15–16, 152–157
Natural Language Understanding (NLU) 16, 155–156
Nauru 109
Nauruan 102
negative face 159, 162
neologisms 53
New York 5, 32
New Zealand 34, 39, 57, 112
Nigerian Pidgin English 86
Nomlaki 113
non-standard 32–33, 141
NORMs 5
noun phrase 28, 77, 173
Nuu-chah-nulth 74

Oakland 127
observer's paradox 23, 40
octopus test 151–152, 156
Ojibwe 77
one language, one nation ideology 51–52
online communication 51, 149, 159–163
onset cluster 116
Orchid Island 116
Ottoman Empire 102
overt prestige 33, 50

Pacific Northwest 74
palatalisation 116
Palo Alto 41, 125
Papua New Guinea 73–74, 84, 89
Papuan languages 98
parliament 49, 124
past tense 115
Patuá 85
perception 30–31, 35, 116
performative speech 116
Persian 7, 48
Peru 115
Philadelphia 34, 141
Philippines 26, 55–56, 76, 90
phonetic 29, 34, 36, 81, 134, 142
phonological variant 22, 25, 37, 41, 116
phonology 25
phonology 29, 66, 160
pidgin 9–10, 33, 36, 72–78, 81, 84–90
Pitkern 75
plantation 10, 75–76, 80
plosive 1, 173
politeness theory 159, 162
Portuguese 10, 82–83, 85, 88, 157

positive face 159, 162
prefix 26, 173
prestige 32, 33, 102
production 15, 23, 31, 37, 39, 115–116, 166
proto-pidgin 84
Punjabi 50

qualitative 7, 9, 16, 166
quantitative 7, 16, 89, 166
Quechua 115

racism 103, 127–128
rate of endangerment 97
Reading 28
real-time 36
Received Pronunciation 36, 156
reconstruction 12, 84
refinedness 116–117
register 6, 40–41
relexification 81
retroflection 39, 173
Réunion Creole 84
reversing language shift 13, 111
rhoticity 5, 26, 32, 173
rural 5, 22, 115
Russia 129
Russian Empire 103

San Francisco 30, 39
Scotland 57
Scottish Gaelic 57
semantic broadening 160
sentiment analysis 15, 155
sequential acquisition 58
Seselwa 85
Sesotho 128
sex 33–35, 37, 122
Seychelles 85
Sierra Leone Krio 75

simultaneous acquisition 58
Singapore 30, 37, 49, 54–56, 87, 130, 142–143
Singapore English 1–2, 15, 25, 29, 37, 49
Sinhala 82
siPuthi 128
slavery 75, 76, 79, 81
Slavey Jargon 74
social factors 3, 31
social justice 125–126, 136
social media 15, 51, 155, 160, 162–163
social network 37–39
social networking platforms 159–163
socioeconomic class 5, 25, 31–33, 43, 60
sociolect 4
sociolinguistic interview 23–24, 115, 166
sociolinguistics 3
solidarity 33, 42, 99
sound symbolism 29
Southern China 9, 76, 88
Southern Min 54, 143
Spanish 52, 75, 87, 127–128
speech community 39
speech recognition 15–16, 153, 157
Sri Lanka Malay 82
St. Lucian Creole French 88
Standard American English 4, 16, 22, 156–157
Standard British English 4, 26, 157
Standard Malay 8
status planning 55
structural borrowing 66
style 6, 32, 40–42, 159
style-shifting 32, 41–42
substrate language 80–82, 89
substrate transfer 80

subtractive bilingualism 59
Sumerian 11
superstrate language 80–82, 89
Swahili 63
Switzerland 3, 48, 116
syntax 4, 27–28, 111

taboo 129
Tahiti 75
Taipei 39
Taiwan 82, 116
Tamil 35–37, 54, 56, 82, 143
tapped /r/ 25–26, 37, 173
Thailand 35, 113, 129, 131
theatre 39–85
Theory of Mind 8
threatened language 11, 85, 87–88, 97, 100, 104, 106, 114
Tobati 98
Tok Pisin 10, 73–74, 84, 86, 89
Tokyo University of Foreign Studies Asian Language Parallel Corpus (TALPCo) 29
transcription 15, 34, 111, 139–143
translanguaging 9, 64–65, 161
translation 29, 86, 123, 128, 136, 143, 153–154
trilled /r/ 25–26, 173
Tsotsitaal 90
Tupari subfamily 104
Tupi 76
Tupían 104
Turing test 149–150, 152

Ubyk 103
Ukraine 149
UNESCO's vitality factors 106–107
United Kingdom 14, 130, 135, 142

United States 7, 33, 48, 52, 77, 126–127, 130, 132–133, 138–140
Universal Declaration of Human Rights 122–123
Universal Declaration of Linguistic Rights 123
urban 6, 90, 115
uvular 115

Valley Girl 4
variation 5, 6, 22–43, 114–117, 135, 156–157
velar 39, 173
verb phrase 77
vernacularisation 75
vocal fry 164, 172
voiced sounds 29, 173
voiceless 30, 173
vowel 29–30, 39, 164–165
vulnerable languages 109

West African languages 75, 87, 157
working class 28, 32, 33
Wu Chinese 102

Xavante 98

Yaghan 11
Yami 116
Yélî Dnye 98
Yiddish 4, 49
Yilan Creole 82

For Product Safety Concerns and Information please contact our EU representative GPSR@taylorandfrancis.com
Taylor & Francis Verlag GmbH, Kaufingerstraße 24, 80331 München, Germany

www.ingramcontent.com/pod-product-compliance
Lightning Source LLC
Chambersburg PA
CBHW052134010526
44113CB00036B/2143